Polar Explorers

Polar Explorers

Other Books in the History Makers Series:

*History*MAKERS

Polar
Explorers

By Stephen Currie

LUCENT BOOKS
SAN DIEGO, CALIFORNIA

THOMSON

GALE

Detroit • New York • San Diego • San Francisco
Boston • New Haven, Conn. • Waterville, Maine
London • Munich

On cover: Robert Peary's exploration team at the North Pole (back-ground); Explorer Richard Byrd holding sundial (upper left); Ernest Shackleton (lower right); Robert Peary (upper right).

Library of Congress Cataloging-in-Publication Data

Currie, Stephen, 1960–
    Polar explorers / by Stephen Currie.
       p. cm. — (History makers)
    Includes bibliographical references (p.) and index.
    Summary: Discusses the lives, education, successes, and failures
of such explorers as John Franklin, Robert Peary, Matthew Henson,
Roald Amundsen, and Robert Falcon Scott as they ventured into the
Arctic and Antarctic.
    ISBN 1-56006-957-0 (hardback : alk. paper)
    1. Explorers—Polar regions—Biography—Juvenile literature.
2. Polar regions—Discovery and exploration—Juvenile literature.
[1. Explorers—Polar regions. 2. Polar regions—Discovery and
exploration.] I. Title. II. Series.
    G584 .C87 2002
    919.804—dc21   2001005783

CONTENTS

The literary form most often referred to as "multiple biography" was perfected in the first century A.D. by Plutarch, a perceptive and talented moralist and historian who hailed from the small town of Chaeronea in central Greece. His most famous work, *Parallel Lives*, consists of a long series of biographies of noteworthy ancient Greek and Roman statesmen and military leaders. Frequently, Plutarch compares a famous Greek to a famous Roman, pointing out similarities in personality and achievements. These expertly constructed and very readable tracts provided later historians and others, including playwrights like Shakespeare, with priceless information about prominent ancient personages and also inspired new generations of writers to tackle the multiple biography genre.

The Lucent History Makers series proudly carries on the venerable tradition handed down from Plutarch. Each volume in the series consists of a set of five to eight biographies of important and influential historical figures who were linked together by a common factor. In *Rulers of Ancient Rome*, for example, all the figures were generals, consuls, or emperors of either the Roman Republic or Empire; while the subjects of *Fighters Against American Slavery*, though they lived in different places and times, all shared the same goal, namely the eradication of human servitude. Mindful that politicians and military leaders are not (and never have been) the only people who shape the course of history, the editors of the series have also included representatives from a wide range of endeavors, including scientists, artists, writers, philosophers, religious leaders, and sports figures.

Each book is intended to give a range of figures—some well known, others less known; some who made a great impact on history, others who made only a small impact. For instance, by making Columbus's initial voyage possible, Spain's Queen Isabella I, featured in *Women Leaders of Nations*, helped to open up the New World to exploration and exploitation by the European powers. Unarguably, therefore, she made a major contribution to a series of events that had momentous consequences for the entire world. By contrast, Catherine II, the eighteenth-century Russian queen, and Golda Meir, the modern Israeli prime minister, did not play roles of global impact; however, their policies and actions significantly influenced the historical development of both their own countries and their regional neighbors. Regardless of their relative importance in the greater historical scheme, all of the figures chronicled in the History Makers series made contributions to posterity; and their public achievements, as well as what is known about their private lives, are presented and evaluated in light of the most recent scholarship.

In addition, each volume in the series is documented and substantiated by a wide array of primary and secondary source quotations. The primary source quotes enliven the text by presenting eyewitness views of the times and culture in which each history maker lived; while the secondary source quotes, taken from the works of respected modern scholars, offer expert elaboration and/or critical commentary. Each quote is footnoted, demonstrating to the reader exactly where biographers find their information. The footnotes also provide the reader with the means of conducting additional research. Finally, to further guide and illuminate readers, each volume in the series features photographs, two bibliographies, and a comprehensive index.

The History Makers series provides both students engaged in research and more casual readers with informative, enlightening, and entertaining overviews of individuals from a variety of circumstances, professions, and backgrounds. No doubt all of them, whether loved or hated, benevolent or cruel, constructive or destructive, will remain endlessly fascinating to each new generation seeking to identify the forces that shaped their world.

A Heroic Age of Exploration

The "Golden Age" of polar exploration lasted through much of the nineteenth century and into the early part of the twentieth. The age was marked by a number of important expeditions to both the Arctic and the Antarctic, sponsored by several different nations. Although many of these voyages were disastrous, many more were tremendously successful. During this time, it seemed as if every year brought news of at least one marvelous new achievement. Expeditions pushed ever closer to the North and South Poles themselves; explorers wintered in the area for two, three, or even four years; voyagers covered astonishing amounts of territory with remarkable speed.

The Golden Age has also been called the Heroic Age, because the men who undertook these explorations often appeared to be larger than life. In a time before instant communication and widespread air travel, they were quite literally heading into the unknown—and would stay away from civilization for months or even years. Their countrymen applauded them for their courage and daring, and their occupation was seen as the ultimate in romantic adventure and drama. These explorers captured the public's attention as sports and entertainment celebrities do today; they were truly heroes of their time.

The list of men who took part in Heroic Age expeditions is long and varied. Some were naval officers, some traders, others self-taught experts in polar travel. Similarly, they hailed from several different countries and headed in various directions. Most were intriguing figures who went on equally compelling voyages. The stories of Norwegian Fridtjof Nansen, Americans Elisha Kent Kane and Adolphus Greely, and Englishman Ernest Shackleton are just some of the ones well worth telling.

But the five Heroic Age explorers whose lives and works are described in this book stand out. All five focused most of their energies on polar objectives, unlike several other explorers of the

An Antarctic glacier. Early polar explorers were fascinated by the harsh adventures awaiting them at the top and bottom of the world.

time who also investigated other parts of the globe. All five concentrated on one or more of the three great polar destinations of the time: the North Pole, the South Pole, or the Northwest Passage. Finally, all five had an unshakable certainty that they knew how to handle the polar regions. Some were right in this belief; others were not. The polar explorers' ability to understand their environment often determined the odds that their expeditions would be a success—and explained their eventual fates.

CHAPTER 1

The Arctic and the Antarctic

For many centuries, the least well-known parts of the world were the polar regions: the Arctic at the far northern tip of the globe, the Antarctic at the southern. Only a relative handful of people lived anywhere near these areas, and those who did lived along the fringes. The rest of the world avoided the polar zones. Bitterly cold in the winter and not much warmer in the summer, the Arctic and the Antarctic seas and landscapes were so choked with ice they seemed impassable.

Most people also did not see any good reason to venture into these areas. As far as Europeans were concerned, the polar regions were frozen wastelands with little value. For centuries, the only travelers in the area were sailors who were blown off course or an occasional hunter in search of whales or seals. Until well into the 1500s, the polar regions remained almost completely unexplored.

The Poles

The best-known features of the polar regions are, of course, the poles themselves. The North and South Poles are not marked by nature, however. No sign, rock, or other geographical structure indicates their location. Instead, the poles are the ends of an imaginary line running north to south through the earth. This line is called the earth's axis. The earth spins, or rotates, as it travels around the sun, and the axis is the line around which it spins. The notion of an axis is an old one; it has proved extremely useful in describing the motion of the earth in and through space.

The globe is also covered by imaginary lines of latitude, which run east and west around the earth. The lines are numbered. The numbering begins at the equator, halfway between the poles, and increases with the distance from the equator. The North Pole lies at latitude 90 degrees north; the South Pole, similarly, is at 90 degrees south. As they approach the poles, the lines of latitude become shorter. At the poles themselves, the length of the line is zero.

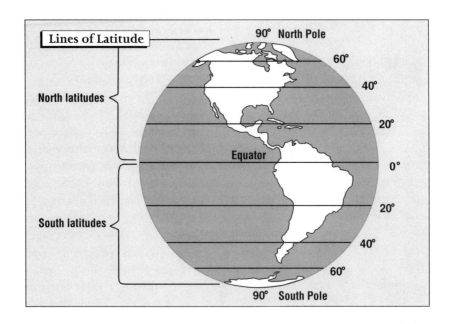

Although there are no markings on the earth's surface, it is possible for an explorer to determine his or her latitude by looking at the stars or measuring the height of the sun above the horizon. Today, technology has made this a relatively easy task, but in the early days of polar exploration it was much more complicated. To find the distance of the sun above the horizon, explorers used instruments such as the sextant, a device made up of a telescope, a mirror, and a curved measuring scale. Making these observations was a complicated and time-consuming task, especially in the bitter cold. Then the travelers would have to make some complex calculations to determine their exact positions.

The North Pole is the center of the Arctic, just as the South Pole is the center of the Antarctic. But the polar regions extend hundreds of miles away from the poles themselves. For some purposes, the Arctic is considered to be everything lying north of the so-called Arctic Circle, another imaginary line near 66 degrees north latitude. Using that definition, the Arctic encompasses all the territory within about sixteen hundred miles of the pole. There is a similar Antarctic Circle the same number of degrees south of the equator.

Other definitions of the polar regions rely less on latitude markings. The Arctic, for example, can also be defined as the place north of the tree line, where the weather is too cold and harsh for trees to grow. That line may be north or south of the Arctic Circle. And the phrase "the Antarctic" is often taken to mean the continent of Antarctica and the stretches of ocean immediately

The first polar explorers used a sextant as a navigational tool.

surrounding it, a definition that likewise does not precisely match the latitude of the Antarctic Circle.

The Regions

In several ways, the two polar regions of the world are much alike. Most obviously, both the Arctic and the Antarctic are extremely cold places. The earth is oriented in space so that sunlight shines most directly onto the areas near the equator; in simple terms, these parts of the earth are always beneath the sun. Conversely, the equator lies a long way from the poles, so the Arctic and Antarctic receive only indirect sunlight. The polar sun never rises very high in the sky, and its warming powers are not strong. Temperatures in the polar regions are the lowest on earth. Indeed, near the poles, year-round ice cover is the rule.

Another similarity involves day and night. At the equator, day and night are exactly the same length no matter what time of year. Farther away from the equator, however, the length of the day varies according to the season. This is carried to an extreme in the Arctic and the Antarctic. In polar regions, the sun stays up for days at a time during the summer and sets for an equal number of days during the winter. At these farthest north and south points on the globe, there is just one sunrise and one sunset a year.

A third similarity between the polar regions involves wildlife. Although no plants or animals exist naturally at the poles, the fringes of both the Arctic and Antarctic are far from barren. The rocky crags of Antarctica are home to several species of penguins, and polar bears live along Arctic coastlines. The polar seas are filled with walruses, seals, whales, and fish. There is plant life, too, especially in the Arctic: mosslike lichens, short hardy grasses, and small flowering plants.

There are differences between the Arctic and Antarctic as well. The most notable is what lies below the icy surface. The center of the north polar region is the Arctic Ocean. Thus, the Arctic is mainly water—usually ice-covered—surrounded by land. In contrast, the south polar region consists mostly of the continent of Antarctica. In a reverse image of the Arctic, this landmass is surrounded by water—the southernmost parts of the Indian, Pacific, and Atlantic Oceans.

A reversal of seasons represents another difference between the two polar zones. What is summer in the Northern Hemisphere is winter in the Southern. In the Arctic, spring arrives in April or May, and sunlight continues through August or September. In Antarctica, the opposite is true. The height of the Antarctic summer occurs during December, January, and February—the winter months in the Northern Hemisphere.

Still another difference involves the residence of people. Some people do live at the edges of the Arctic. Most notable among these small populations are the Inuit, often called Eskimos, whose territory extends from Greenland to Siberia, including all of northern North America. On the other hand, no one lives permanently in the southern polar region. Antarctica is too barren for survival, and the nearest settlements—at the southern tip of South America—are too far north to be truly "Antarctic."

Early Explorers

For many years, most of this information was unknown. Except for a few southern stretches of the Arctic, the map of the northern

An August sun is pictured at the geographic North Pole. During the Arctic summer, the sun shines for days before it sets.

polar zone was a complete blank. The Vikings had established a colony in southern Greenland, but no Europeans had penetrated much farther into the ice. As for the Antarctic, no one knew anything about it. Voyages toward the area were rare.

Indeed, for centuries, no one knew for certain what the top and bottom of the world were like. Several people theorized that the Arctic Ocean was warm, though surrounded by a ring of ice, and that a ship which could get through the ice would find smooth sailing. Others suggested that the earth was hollow and that the South Pole would prove to connect to the interior of the globe. Since no one had visited either part of the world at the time, no one could prove them wrong.

The modern age of Arctic exploration began in the 1500s with a series of voyages undertaken for commercial reasons. Silk, spices, and other goods produced in the Far East were popular in Europe. But the distance between Europe and Asia was great, and existing land and sea routes were long and circuitous. The most common sea route, for instance, was around the southern tip of Africa, a voyage that could take many weeks. High prices were necessary to support the costs of shipment, which meant that these goods were expensive and hard to obtain in Europe.

Governments and business interests all hoped to find quicker, shorter routes to Asia. Whoever discovered such a path would reap the benefits of increased trade with the countries of the Far East. Attention began to turn to the Arctic as a possible route. Ideally, explorers agreed, it would prove possible to sail along the northern coasts without getting caught in the ice. Once in the northern Pacific Ocean, a ship could sail south through more temperate waters and reach the Asian trading ports in less time than other routes would take.

Passages

There were two possible Arctic routes from Europe. The first was called the Northeast Passage, which curled north of Norway and continued east over the northern boundary of Russia. This route was favored by the Dutch government, which offered a reward to any sea captain who could sail through the passage and demonstrate its usefulness. The Dutch, at the time, were perhaps the most active traders in Europe, and speed of travel to Asia was quite important to them.

Among those who tried to collect the reward was a Dutch sailor named Willem Barents. Barents's first two attempts were unsuccessful. There was simply too much ice in the northern channels,

16

and the summer season was far too short to give it time to melt. On his third journey, Barents's ship was trapped in floating ice. The men were forced to spend the winter on an Arctic island, where they constructed a basic shelter from driftwood and a sail from the ship. Barents himself died of scurvy before the men could return to civilization, but several members of his party survived the experience—the first Europeans to do so. Their story demonstrated that the Arctic might well be impassable, even brutal. But even at its worst, it was not necessarily fatal.

The Dutch also looked west to the so-called Northwest Passage across the top of North America. So, too, did the English, another great seafaring nation. Henry Hudson found the Hudson River and Hudson Bay while looking for the passage. Martin Frobisher cruised western Greenland and encountered the Inuit, whom he described as "strange infidels [that is, non-Christians] whose like was never seen, read, nor heard of before."[1] William Baffin searched farther north still, reaching a latitude of 78 degrees north.

Many of these expeditions brought back important information about the Arctic, but none achieved their main goal: finding a navigable northeast or northwest passage. Explorers and governments grew discouraged. Between the early 1600s and the late

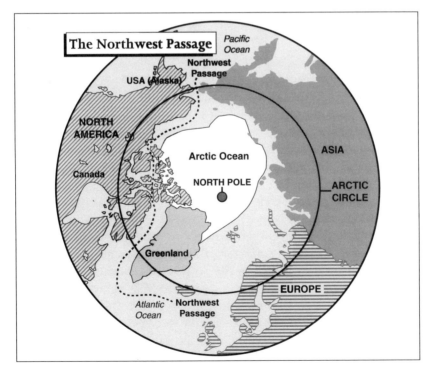

Although British sea captain James Cook did not discover Antarctica, his multiple crossings of the Antarctic Circle left him certain that a continent existed in the region.

1700s, several explorers made their way into the floating ice of the Arctic, but most people turned their attention elsewhere. In any case, no one traveled much beyond the marks set by Baffin, Frobisher, or Barents.

The Antarctic

In the late eighteenth century, Europe at last became interested in the much more distant Antarctic. British sea captain James Cook was among the first to cross the Antarctic Circle, which he did several times on one voyage beginning in 1772. He would eventually reach latitude 71 degrees south before heading north again. In Cook's opinion, the Antarctic seas were dreadful. The waves were treacherous, the icebergs immense, and the cold "so intense as hardly to be endured."[2]

Cook came away from the experience convinced that the Antarctic seas surrounded a continent. Actually finding it, though, would have to wait a generation or two. In 1820, Nathaniel Palmer of the United States spotted the tip of the Antarctic Peninsula, a ribbon of land protruding north of the Antarctic Circle. That was the first sighting of Antarctica, although no one knew it at the time. A year later, the Russian Fabian Bellingshausen discovered several islands within the Antarctic Circle—the southernmost points of land anyone had ever seen.

Little by little, explorers penetrated farther south. By the 1840s, much of the continent's coastline had been mapped and explored.

English explorer James Clark Ross traveled to both the Antarctic continent and the Arctic region.

Most of the work had been done from the sea, but a few expeditions had gone onshore, most notably one led by Englishman James Clark Ross in 1841. It had become abundantly clear that Antarctica was indeed a continent.

Like the exploration of the Arctic, the exploration of the southern polar regions was sparked partly by economic reasons. The southern seas were not a gateway to anything, but many Europeans believed that the continent itself harbored wealth. The seals and whales were of particular interest to hunters; indeed, Nathaniel Palmer, one of Antarctica's early discoverers, was a sealer. Moreover, they believed there might be important minerals in the continent. As with the Northwest and Northeast Passages, the country that found the minerals first could become rich.

Early Antarctic exploration had another important foundation as well: science and geography. Antarctica offered scientists an intriguing laboratory unlike any other spot on earth. Climatologists—those interested in weather—knew that they could learn more about the earth's overall climate and weather patterns from recording the temperatures, snowfall, and winds of the polar regions. Geologists came to study the rocks and the ice, biologists to study the wildlife. For a time, explorers also focused on locating the South Magnetic Pole, the spot to which Southern Hemisphere compasses point.

An increasing number of explorers also longed to fill in missing sections of maps. In part, this was a desire for knowledge for its own sake. But personal glory and national pride were at stake, too. Several different countries were involved in Antarctic research. Even if there was little wealth in being the first country to find the pole or to discover a polar mountain range, there was honor in it.

The Northwest Passage Revisited

In the early nineteenth century, interest in the Northwest Passage had resurfaced. By this time, it was clear that the Northeast Passage would not serve as a valuable route to the Far East. There was simply too much ice. But the route through Canada still seemed possible, and England, in particular, sent out a number of explorers beginning in about 1819.

These expeditions were not motivated primarily by economics. True, it was still barely conceivable that a quicker way to China might appear. But other considerations now played a larger role. Discovering new scientific information about minerals, climate, and magnetism was important to these new explorers, as it was to those who sailed for Antarctica. So was personal glory; explorers vied with each other to see who could make the greatest and most interesting discoveries.

Perhaps most important of all was national pride. England was eager to show off its strength, its know-how, and its ingenuity, and the country's leaders could think of no better path to glory than to send ships into the Canadian Arctic. As an English official said, it would be "somewhat mortifying"[3] if another country, such as Russia, managed to navigate the passage first—especially given that the English had begun exploring the area three centuries earlier.

None of these expeditions achieved their stated goal. The Canadian Arctic consists of a great many islands divided by a maze of waterways. Some of these channels are many miles across, while others are quite narrow. Finding a way through the network was time-consuming and frustrating. An explorer might follow a broad waterway between two islands only to discover that the other end was choked with ice. Other promising routes turned out to be bays or fjords reaching deep into the mainland. The Northwest Passage remained elusive through the 1830s, although explorers still hoped that a path through the maze could be found.

In other ways, however, the Arctic expeditions of the early nineteenth century were very successful. Many of these explorers carried out important scientific and geographical research. James Clark Ross, who also traveled to Antarctica, located the North Magnetic Pole. William Edward Parry sailed through much of the eastern Canadian Arctic, mapping as he went, and took a side journey north to within eight degrees of the North Pole itself.

For the first time, too, Arctic expeditions began to spend winters in the polar regions. Unlike William Barents, these explorers did so by choice, not by accident. The distances to be traveled were simply too far to cover in one summer, so expeditions prepared to be iced in. A few survived reasonably well. Others ran into major difficulties, typically involving disease, insufficient shelter, or dwindling supplies. Either way, the men were willing to try. The Golden Age of polar exploration was now well under way. The polar regions—and the poles themselves—would remain a tempting goal for several generations of explorers to come.

CHAPTER 2

John Franklin

The early nineteenth-century explorer most famous for his work in the Arctic is English naval officer John Franklin. Well known and widely admired during his own time, Franklin continues to be remembered today. A member of four polar expeditions and the leader of three, Franklin explored and mapped many unknown miles of Arctic coastlines during his voyages. At a time when very little was known about the Canadian Arctic, Franklin brought courage and enthusiasm to a series of dangerous assignments.

Franklin's legacy is mixed, however. He showed poor judgment in his leadership of at least one expedition, and his fourth and final voyage ended in complete disaster. Despite his strengths and achievements, Franklin never grasped the harsh realities of Arctic travel. Too often, he persisted in seeing polar conditions as only a little bit fiercer than what prevailed in Britain. As a result, he tried to handle them just as he would have done elsewhere in the civilized world. In the end, these miscalculations led to tragedy.

In his assertions, however, Franklin was very much a creation of his time. Many English explorers of the early 1800s shared similar notions. So did members of the British government. In their view, the technical prowess of Europeans was stronger than the hazards of the natural world. England could, and would, subdue the Arctic; what is more, it would do so without specialized training or equipment especially adapted to polar conditions. On occasion—as with Franklin's third voyage—the determination and drive inherent in this approach led to great success. But when English bravado failed, as it did on Franklin's final journey, the scope of the disaster was enormous.

Early Years

John Franklin was born in Spilsby, England, in 1786, the youngest son in a family of eight children. The family was well-off and valued education, and young John's parents hoped to send him to Oxford University. One of his brothers had already attended classes there. However, John had other ideas. Some of his relatives were seamen, and he found himself drawn to a life aboard a ship.

Arctic explorer John Franklin entered the British navy as a midshipman at age fifteen.

His parents did not stand in his way. They kept him in school until he was twelve, and then allowed him to join one of his uncles, who was a sea captain. Three years later, Franklin officially joined the Royal Navy with the beginning rank of midshipman. If all went well for him, he could expect to rise rather quickly through the ranks, perhaps becoming a commanding officer in his twenties.

At first, things did indeed go well. Barely fifteen years old, he served aboard the HMS *Polyphemus* during the Battle of Copenhagen in 1801, part of the Napoleonic Wars and a major victory for the British forces against the Danes. Two years later, Franklin served aboard another ship that sailed around Australia, proving that it was a continent. In 1805, Franklin returned to the Napoleonic Wars. At the Battle of Trafalgar, Franklin served aboard the *Bellerophon*, which saw very heavy action during yet another British victory.

These early postings were perfect assignments for an ambitious young sailor. They provided ample opportunity for Franklin to shine and rise quickly through the ranks. But even though Franklin served capably during these years, he seemed to have little initiative. He also did not have much of a taste for fighting. His friends noted that he would not even kill a fly: "The world is wide enough for both,"[4] he often said. Instead of battles, Franklin became interested in the technical specialties of navigation and surveying—neither of which was on the fast track to promotion.

To be sure, Franklin did have great strengths as a sailor and as a man. He got along well with nearly everyone. He loved his parents and siblings and wrote home often; he was charming and friendly to friends and strangers alike. He was also an optimist. On the Australian voyage, for example, he and some companions had been shipwrecked on the Great Barrier Reef. They had been forced to live on a small island for many weeks until they could be rescued. Despite the difficult situation, Franklin never gave up hope. "We shall be [away] from this bank in six or eight weeks," he wrote in his journal, exuding complete confidence, "and most probably in England by eight or nine."[5]

To the Arctic

In 1818, Franklin was given a new and interesting assignment. Sir John Barrow, a British naval official of the time, was planning an expedition to try to reach the North Pole. Barrow ordered a captain named David Buchan to take two ships to the Norwegian island of Spitsbergen, north of the mainland. From there, Barrow instructed the voyagers to follow channels of water northward through the pack ice. Franklin was appointed second-in-command.

The travelers left on schedule, but soon found that the work was harder than Barrow had thought. There were indeed a few pathways through the ice, but they quickly became too narrow to navigate. "The channels by degrees disappeared," wrote one crewman, "and the ice, with its accustomed rapidity, soon became packed, encircled the vessels and pressed so closely upon them that one boundless plain of rugged snow extended in every direction."[6] Barrow had hoped that the ice simply surrounded a warm and easily navigable polar sea; evidently, however, this was not the case.

In desperation, the crews poured out onto the surrounding ice and tried to drag the ships through with ropes and chains. When dragging the ships did not work, Buchan promptly sailed back to Spitsbergen and then to England. Today it is known that his task had been impossible: Sailing to the pole was out of the question. Still, Buchan had returned too quickly and given up too easily to suit Barrow. Thus, when Barrow decided to launch another Arctic expedition the following year, he passed over Buchan and gave the role of commander to Buchan's chief assistant: John Franklin.

In Command

Barrow had clear ideas of what he wanted from this second expedition. First, he ordered Franklin and his men to sail across the Atlantic and into Hudson Bay in Canada. The expedition would then make its way across the northern Canadian wilderness on foot and by canoe. Eventually, Barrow expected the travelers to arrive at the Arctic Ocean and spend some time surveying the coastline to the east. Some of the land they would cover had already been mapped and explored, but much of it had not; doing so would be Franklin's chief responsibility.

Although Franklin had some polar experience, he was not well qualified to lead the expedition Barrow had in mind. He was much more at home on large ships than in the smaller canoes the travelers would need, and he had no experience hunting or backpacking. He also lacked the build or the muscles necessary for successful work in the Arctic. "Lieut. Franklin," wrote one man with Canadian Arctic experience, "has not the physical powers required for the labor of moderate Voyaging in this country. . . . With the utmost exertion he cannot walk Eight miles in one day."[7]

Franklin (holding rifle, center) is pictured on kayaks with a crew, supplies, and dogs around 1818.

Franklin, however, was determined to make the most of his opportunity. He chose three other young British naval officers to be part of his group. He also hired several Canadian voyageurs, which was important since these strong men were accustomed to canoeing in the wilderness. They would do most of the paddling and heavy lifting. Finally, Franklin arranged to pay Native Americans to help guide him and his party—and to do any hunting that might be necessary.

In 1819, Franklin left England for Hudson Bay. He arrived at the bay's western end shortly before winter set in. The following summer, he traveled west. North of Great Slave Lake, but still south of the Arctic Circle, Franklin and his men constructed two small houses for shelter; they called the outpost Fort Enterprise. After wintering at Fort Enterprise, Franklin turned north again during the summer of 1821. This time he headed into the Arctic itself.

To the Arctic Ocean

Franklin's path lay along the Coppermine River, which began not far from Fort Enterprise and flowed directly into the Arctic Ocean. The river, unfortunately, was wild and dangerous. It was filled with treacherous rapids, and in many places the men were forced to make portages—to carry the canoes and the supplies to a safer area farther downstream. The going was very slow, and Franklin and the other naval officers were of little help.

After a terrible struggle, the group at last managed to reach the ocean. It would have been wise for Franklin to have stopped there. The season was late, the men were exhausted, and the food supplies were getting dangerously low. A quick return would have been strenuous, but at least they would return to Fort Enterprise before conditions became desperate. Nevertheless, Franklin decided to push east. Those were his orders, and he hoped to complete his task. Having come so far, he could not justify cutting the journey short.

The voyage down the Coppermine had been difficult; the trip along the coastline was a nightmare. The canoes were damaged and nearly destroyed by ocean waves and currents. The Native American hunters could not find enough game to feed all the men, and the food the explorers had brought with them ran out completely. But by the time Franklin realized that he had made a mistake, the men had traveled over a hundred miles eastward from the mouth of the Coppermine.

It was late August. The Arctic summer was at an end, and winter was on its way. Fort Enterprise now lay more than three hundred miles off. The men tried to paddle back to the Coppermine in their battered canoes, but could not make it. As a result, the travelers were forced to make their way to Fort Enterprise on foot.

The snow and cold of early winter soon made travel extremely difficult. "Our tents were completely frozen," wrote Franklin in his journal that September, "and the snow had drifted around them to a depth of three feet."[8] Worse than the weather was exhaustion. By this time, the men had worked themselves so hard that they could barely continue. But the biggest problem was food. With absolutely nothing left and little opportunity to hunt, the men were forced to eat lichens and even pieces of their own shoes.

The expedition was saved, though barely. Most of the men managed to stumble back to Fort Enterprise. Several of Franklin's native

Franklin survived the desperate journey back to Fort Enterprise; eleven of his men perished.

guides were still in the area, having been left there to await the travelers' return. The travelers met up with the guides just in time; by all accounts, most of Franklin's men were at most a day or two from death. The guides fed the men and nursed many of them back to health. Franklin was among the explorers who survived. However, eleven of the men did die, some along the trail and others in Fort Enterprise.

Though total disaster had been averted, the expedition was hardly a success. It was somewhat to Franklin's surprise, then, when he returned home to find himself hailed as a hero. In the popular mind, he had taken on the mighty Arctic and survived. More than that, the English argued, accounts of the journey showed that Franklin and his men had showed remarkable courage and resourcefulness, as evidenced in part when the men had eaten their shoes.

Certainly, Franklin had survived some truly dreadful experiences, and his expedition had mapped many miles of the Arctic. But Franklin's command had been problematic. His leadership had often been wanting. He had pushed on when he should have played it safe, and he had absolutely failed to pay proper attention to the food supplies and the health of his men. His pride in following his orders surpassed his caution and common sense. Moreover, the real heroes of the expedition were the voyageurs and the Indians; the voyageurs, after all, had done most of the paddling and carrying, and the Indians had hunted and saved the survivors at the end of the trip. But deservedly or not, Franklin was considered a hero.

Marriage

After he returned home, Franklin began to court a well-known poet named Eleanor Porden. The courtship, however, seems to have been mainly on Porden's part. The two kept up a long correspondence, during which she wrote him long, lively letters to which he replied only occasionally. In 1822 Franklin asked Porden to marry, but evidently did so with such lack of enthusiasm and passion that at first she refused. When they at last did agree to marry, he waited five months before telling his friends and family of the engagement. One historian described the engagement, from Franklin's side at least, as containing "about as much heat as afternoon tea."[9]

The marriage was not an especially happy one for either member of the couple. The two were quite different. Eleanor was witty and sophisticated; John, despite his extensive travels, was neither. Eleanor had deep doubts about religion; John was a devout Christian who was faintly appalled by his wife's attitude. Eleanor was passionate about culture and the arts; John had no interest in them at all. "Captn. Franklin told me he had never been [to an opera]," remarked one friend, "and did not think he could sit it out."[10] Eleanor gave birth to a daughter, also named Eleanor, but even before then it was clear that the two were sadly incompatible.

Franklin was already looking past the marriage. His greatest desire was to return to the Arctic, and with his new fame he was sure it would not be difficult. That was especially true since Franklin had the support and admiration of Barrow. Over the next two years, the two men discussed a third Arctic voyage to northern Canada, this one to be larger and longer than the one along the Coppermine. Franklin again would command the expedition; after his previous voyage, he was now acknowledged as the greatest Arctic explorer in Britain.

Planning for the next expedition was complicated and time-consuming, but Franklin was finally ready to leave in 1825. During this period, his wife of barely two years had fallen quite ill with tuberculosis. It was evident that she was near death, but Franklin knew that the voyage could not be put off for even a few days without running the risk of having to wait an entire year. The Arctic summer was so short that the explorers had only a narrow window of opportunity for safe, ice-free travel.

Choosing to leave Eleanor behind, Franklin set sail in February. He brought with him a flag that she had made, having promised to unfurl it on the Arctic coastline once he reached it. Despite the struggles in their marriage, Franklin wrote his wife almost daily from the time he left. The letters were to no avail: Six days after his departure, Eleanor Porden Franklin died, leaving their daughter in Franklin's sister Isabella's charge. Her husband, however, did not hear the news for nearly two months.

Success

Franklin's third voyage was by far his most successful. On this journey, Franklin reached Great Slave Lake without incident and then headed northwest along the Mackenzie River. This trek was easier and faster than the trip down the Coppermine had been. On August 16, 1825, he reached the Arctic Ocean and planted the flag his wife had given him. Then he and his men quickly retreated inland to set up winter quarters before the good weather was completely gone. This time, Franklin made sure not to skimp on food supplies. "[We] have our breakfast directly [upon rising]," he reported, "dinner at half-past five, and tea at nine."[11]

In June 1826, the men were off again. Franklin traveled back down the Mackenzie to the Arctic coastline. There, he divided the company into two parts. He assigned his friend John Richardson to explore the coastline to the east, taking some of the men with him. The remaining explorers followed Franklin to the west. If all went well, Franklin's group would travel through the western section of the Northwest Passage and meet up with a British ship stationed off the Alaskan coast.

Franklin and his group made excellent time at first. That August, however, they ran into bad weather. North of Alaska and running out of time, Franklin was forced to decide whether to press on or to turn back. This time, faced with potential danger, he chose to return to safety. Richardson's men made it back to camp without difficulty, too. All in all, the expedition had been remarkably successful. No one had died; in fact, no one had even come close. Franklin had mapped six hundred miles of unexplored coastline, and Richardson had contributed another thousand. In 1827, the men returned home to cheers.

Once home, Franklin began to court Jane Griffin, a friend of Eleanor's whom he had known for some time. Griffin had already

Second wife Jane Griffin was very supportive of Franklin's endeavors.

turned down several marriage proposals, but she found Franklin irresistible. Within a year, the two were married. This time, Franklin believed, he had found a soulmate. "There exists between us the closest congeniality of mind, thought and feeling,"[12] he wrote her father.

Nevertheless, the two women were similar. Like Eleanor, Jane was an unusually intelligent woman who cared little for tradition and prided herself on being an independent thinker. Jane was also quite different from her husband. In great contrast to John's single-minded pursuit of Arctic exploration, she threw herself into social and intellectual activities of all kinds. Whereas John was shy and easygoing, she was opinionated and ambitious. Yet this time the marriage was a clear success. John doted on Jane, and she in turn loved and supported him in his polar pursuits.

Disappointment

At this point, the only major section of the Northwest Passage remaining unexplored was a five-hundred-mile stretch east of the Coppermine. A well-stocked and carefully chosen expedition, Franklin reasoned, should easily be able to manage to traverse the entire passage. Unfortunately for Franklin, naval budgets were shrinking rapidly. Franklin was not invited to return to the Arctic. Instead, he was given a different assignment—full command of a ship posted in the Mediterranean Sea.

Franklin was lucky to have a job at all. Many of his fellow officers were put "on the beach," an expression that meant being taken off active duty altogether and given only half pay. Indeed, his Mediterranean command was considered a prime posting. Still, Franklin was not satisfied. For three years he chafed at the assignment and wished he were nearer his beloved Arctic. Finally, at the urging of Jane, he asked naval leaders for a new assignment. "Your shy, timid husband must have gathered some brass [bravery]," he wrote of himself to Jane, "or you will be at a loss to account for his extraordinary courage."[13]

Courageous or not, Franklin did not get his request. Instead, naval officials responded by putting Franklin himself on the beach. After two years, the navy contacted him again and offered him a post as governor of the Caribbean island of Antigua. Franklin refused, evidently holding out for something closer to the Arctic. He was encouraged in his refusal by his wife, who considered Antigua too obscure and the posting not prestigious enough to suit her husband.

A year later, the navy offered Franklin the governorship of Van Diemen's Land, an island off the Australian coast that is now called Tasmania. This time, Franklin accepted the offer. Perhaps he feared that he would never get another decent job. Certainly he was feeling the financial pinch of drawing only half pay. Perhaps most important of all, though, was the opinion of his wife. Jane encouraged him to take the post; she believed it would lead to bigger and better things.

She was wrong. Van Diemen's Land was a rough-and-tumble penal colony. About eighteen thousand English prisoners lived there under heavy guard, along with twenty-four thousand free Englishmen. Franklin did his best to establish gentle ways of dealing with the prisoners; he and his wife also tried to bring culture and religion to the community. Unfortunately, they both stepped on the toes of several of the colonial leaders. These men and women saw the Franklins as intent on changing their cherished way of life. They petitioned for Franklin's recall, and got it. After several extremely difficult years, Franklin, his wife, and his daughter returned to England.

At this point, Franklin's prospects seemed dim. Now fifty-seven, he was a relatively old man who had accomplished very little since his early forties. Worse, he had failed in Van Diemen's Land and was once more on the beach. Franklin was no longer at the forefront of the public mind. Still, he was not through yet. He continued to badger his superiors for another assignment, preferably one that would bring him to the Arctic again, although the odds appeared to be remote at best.

One More Time

However, luck was with Franklin. In 1845, England decided to make one more attempt on the Northwest Passage. Leadership of the expedition was offered at first to James Clark Ross, an Englishman with extensive polar experience. When Ross declined, the prize was then offered to two other men, both younger and fitter than Franklin. They, too, turned down the opportunity.

Talk next turned to Franklin. In Franklin's favor was his experience and his enthusiasm. Against him was his age and the fact that he had not been to the Arctic in more than twenty years. Franklin assured them that he was fit enough for a sailing expedition. Franklin's friend, explorer William Parry, spoke on his behalf. "If you don't let him go," he told naval officials, "the man will die of disappointment."[14] In the end, Franklin was accepted and preparations began.

This expedition was to be huge. Two large state-of-the-art ships, the *Erebus* and the *Terror*, were to carry 134 men into the Canadian wilderness. Franklin was quite sure that he and his men would succeed: Either they would find the Northwest Passage and sail back in triumph, or their exhaustive exploration of the Arctic coastline would reveal that the passage did not exist. The men were well supplied with canned English foods and warm English-made clothing. In Franklin's view, there was no way that the expedition could fail.

Only John Ross, the uncle of James Clark Ross and a veteran explorer himself, seems to have questioned Franklin's plans. He feared that such enormous boats would run aground in the ice-

A picture of John Franklin's expeditionary ships, the Erebus *and the* Terror.

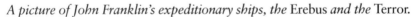

choked shallows of the Arctic. He also worried that so many men would be impossible to feed. In general, too, Ross suspected that Franklin was overconfident. The Arctic, he pointed out, was not easily tamed. "Has anyone volunteered to follow you?"[15] he asked Franklin, suggesting that it would be wise to arrange for a relief ship in case of trouble. But Franklin, in his certainty that he would succeed, laughed off Ross's concerns. After all, a voyage that could not fail would certainly need no rescuing.

In May 1845, the ships left England. Franklin was ecstatic. At last, he had a chance to finish the work he had started more than two decades ago. "Oh, how I wish I could write to every one of them [his relatives]," he wrote his wife, "to assure them of the happiness I feel in my officers, my crew, and my ship!"[16] The expedition stopped in Greenland and then headed across Baffin Bay, where the officers spoke briefly to the captains of two whaling ships. It was the last time any Europeans would see any of the party alive.

Disaster

In 1847, two years after Franklin left, John Ross grew worried. No one had heard from Franklin since that day on Baffin Bay. Ross did not see how such a large expedition could manage to live through three polar winters without some loss of health or life. He proposed to command a voyage to find Franklin and bring him new supplies. But he was flatly turned down. Franklin was fine, naval officials assured him, only biding his time in the frozen Arctic. Besides, if Franklin were in trouble, what could another ship do? "You will go and get frozen in," one official told Ross, "and we shall have to send after you!"[17]

Not until the spring of 1848 did naval leaders begin to show concern. After considering several possible courses of action, the government finally launched an assault on the Arctic from a number of different directions. James Clark Ross was dispatched with two large ships of his own and told to follow Franklin's route. John Richardson, who had mapped part of the Arctic coastline on Franklin's previous expedition, took an overland journey. Two other ships were sent to Alaska to search from the western end of the passage.

But none succeeded. Franklin's voyagers had evidently vanished without a trace. Over the next few years, searchers from the United States and many other nations also joined the fray, though to no avail. The government offered a reward to anyone who could locate Franklin. Jane Franklin enlisted support from much of Europe

The fate of Franklin's ill-fated final voyage was unknown until 1859, when searchers discovered a large pile of stones containing two messages from Franklin.

and North America, tirelessly writing letters to everone she could think of who might be of some help. Years went by, much of the Canadian Arctic was crossed and recrossed, and still no one could find a trace of the missing expedition.

The fate of the explorers remained uncertain until 1859, when searchers reached King William Island in the central Arctic. There they found a six-foot-high pile of stones surrounded by a pile of discarded equipment—tools, blankets, barrel hoops, and much more. Inside the pile of stones was a piece of paper bearing two messages from the Franklin expedition. The first, dated May 1847, gave some information on the journey and reported that all was well.

But the second, dated eleven months later, revealed that disaster had struck. The ships had remained frozen into the ice for nearly two years. The men were abandoning them, the message reported, and heading south across the wilderness—a nine-hundred mile march to the nearest place of refuge that the rescuers knew would have been virtually impossible. The message also gave gruesome statistics. Already the expedition had lost nearly one-fifth of its members. As for Franklin, he had passed away in June 1847, making him among the very first to die.

Aftermath

Exactly what happened to Franklin and his men will never be known, but the basic outline is clear. Once the ships became stuck in the ice off King William Island, supplies dwindled and some men began to grow ill. There were few hunters in the party, and there was little in the way of game for so many people. With no prospect of a relief ship—after all, Franklin had specifically refused one—the men's only hope was to walk to safety. None made it. The voyage ended in death for every member of the expedition.

Part of the blame lay with Franklin himself. He was in no physical shape to lead such a large expedition. He should also have been more willing to admit the possibility of failure, thus accepting Ross's offer of a rescue ship. It would not have saved his own life but might have saved the lives of many of his men. There is little information about Franklin's leadership during this final voyage, but if his earlier trips are any guide, he probably made his share of errors in judgment as a leader.

Although the public considered Franklin a hero, his attempts to find the Northwest Passage ended in failure.

Perhaps a greater share of the blame, though, lay with Barrow and the other navy officials. They had mounted an overly large expedition. They had stocked too-big ships with useless silverware, books, and the like; they had chosen not to send a relief ship even after Ross begged them to do so. Perhaps most important of all, they had believed that a well-trained navy officer could do virtually anything he set his mind to. The fact that a voyage across the Arctic presented very different challenges than fighting on a warship does not seem to have occurred to them.

Franklin was dead, and he died a hero in the popular imagination. Jane Franklin paid for a monument in London's Westminster Abbey. The *New York Times* spoke for many when it called the tragedy "as noble an epic as that which has immortalized the fall of Troy or the conquest of Jerusalem."[18] But in the long run, the expedition was a complete failure. The Northwest Passage had not been found.

John Franklin had the weight of an empire behind him as he crossed into the Canadian Arctic. His ships and his sailors were among the best in the world. He had expert navigators and experienced doctors; he had up-to-date maps and all the provisions he could fit aboard his ships. He had know-how, technical prowess, and science on his side. But nature was stronger.

CHAPTER 3

Robert Peary

Of all the polar explorers, Robert Peary was certainly the most ambitious. "Remember, Mother, I *must* have fame,"[19] he wrote in an early letter. Indeed, Peary devoted much of his life to the single-minded pursuit of a goal: being the first at the North Pole. Blessed—or perhaps cursed—with an abundance of drive, determination, and arrogance, Peary let nothing stand in his way of achieving this goal.

Robert Edwin Peary was born on May 6, 1856, in Cresson, Pennsylvania, but he grew up mostly in Maine. From early on, he was a high achiever who pushed himself to excel. Although he could be rebellious and a practical joker, he was a serious student when the occasion demanded. Peary attended several boarding schools and then went off to Bowdoin College in Brunswick, Maine, where he did extremely well, graduating second in his class with a degree in civil engineering.

Peary's early life was also marked by a certain degree of fear and loneliness. His father died of pneumonia when he was only three, and his mother—whom he loved deeply—was subject to frequent spells of illness, the exact cause of which are unknown today. Peary felt responsible for her, and this sense of responsibility weighed on him. "As mother got up to go to bed," he wrote one night, "she suddenly became very weak and cold on her left side so she could not walk. It scared me very much."[20] Peary immediately rubbed her hands and feet until she felt better. He was only sixteen at the time, and he was all she had. Fortunately, money was not an issue; Peary's father had owned property and left his family fairly well off in his will.

Perhaps in part because of Peary's difficult family situation, he often felt awkward in public settings. Shy and somewhat suspicious of strangers, he was slow to warm up to people. "It is so lonesome," he wrote upon entering college, "that I don't know what to do with myself. All the faces are strange and I seem to be in a distant country."[21] It surely did not help that he could be intensely competitive as well. "I must be the peer or superior of those around me to be comfortable,"[22] he wrote his mother, and his life reflected that intense desire.

Soon after graduating from Bowdoin, Peary moved to Washington, D.C. With his engineering background, he accepted a position as a draftsman with a government agency. Before long he had moved on to the navy's Corps of Engineers, where he joined the service as a lieutenant. Here he became deeply interested in building a canal across Central America, an idea much in vogue among naval officials at the time. Peary thought that building the canal was certainly possible. And more important, he expected that there would be fame in store for the man who accomplished the task; he hoped to be that man.

In 1884, Peary journeyed to Nicaragua to begin surveying the region. His goal was to find an appropriate route for a canal. The work was miserable and slow. The men spent most of their days waist-deep in water, cutting and lifting logs, weeds, and other ob-

Full of determination and ambition—and intensely competitive—Robert Peary was driven to achieve fame.

stacles. "Everyone was thoroughly wet and tired," Peary wrote about one typical day, "having been in the water over ten hours."[23] Peary distinguished himself through his work in Nicaragua, mapping out a shorter route than anyone expected. But the government seemed to have lost interest in the project. To Peary's disappointment, it did not immediately act on his recommendations.

Instead, government officials thanked Peary for a job well done and sent him home to Washington. While mulling over what he should do next, he visited a bookstore, where he ran across an account of a trip to Greenland written by Scandinavian explorer Baron A. E. Nordenskiold. Peary had previously shown little interest in polar exploration, though some biographers believe that during his childhood he probably read and enjoyed the accounts of American explorer Elisha Kent Kane. Now, however, he was hooked.

To Greenland

Peary spent much of the rest of the year reading everything he could find on Arctic exploration. By the end of the fall, he had resolved to make a Greenland trip of his own. This trek would only be a warmup, however. Even then, Peary had little interest in Greenland for itself; his main purpose, instead, was to practice in Arctic conditions and find the best techniques for making an assault on the North Pole.

A careful thinker and a fine student, Peary took copious notes on earlier expeditions. He came away from these studies with clear ideas of efficient polar travel. Most notable, perhaps, was a strong preference for small expeditions. "The old method of large parties and small ships has been run into the ground,"[24] he wrote in his diary, resolving not to follow in any way the example of John Franklin and others who believed that bigger was better.

In the summer of 1886, Peary was ready to begin. He took a leave of absence from the navy and sailed north to the widest part of Greenland. His intent was to cross the island with a Danish companion, thereby becoming the first to do so at that latitude. The two men did not make it; indeed, they barely traveled a hundred miles before returning to their base camp. Polar conditions proved much worse than Peary had anticipated. However, Peary did make the first recorded ascent of part of the Greenland ice cap, and in that way the voyage was a clear success. The fame Peary so desperately sought began to come his way.

Unfortunately, the Greenland expedition raised two significant issues that would dog Peary during the rest of his career. One involved the accuracy of his records. Norwegian explorer Fridtjof

Norwegian explorer Fridtjof Nansen (pictured) was critical of the accuracy of Peary's record-keeping.

Nansen pointed out some problems with Peary's navigational techniques. While Peary was probably close to where he said he was, Nansen argued, he had been sloppy in making observations; thus, Peary could not give his position with certainty.

The other issue involved Peary's reactions to other explorers. He seemed to consider Greenland, and indeed the entire Arctic, his own personal property. Three years after Peary's trip, for example, Nansen crossed Greenland at a somewhat narrower point. Peary did his best to downplay the Norwegian's achievement, at one point even complaining that Nansen had stolen his ideas—although Nansen had published many of his plans well before Peary had begun to consider his first expedition.

Peary was eager to make another trip, but the navy had other ideas. Over the next several years he was assigned to several engineering projects, most of them involving canals and other waterways. In 1888, he was ordered back to Nicaragua, where he returned to work on the proposed canal across Central America. There he took part in surveys and was responsible for fifty workers.

During these years, Peary's strongest emotional connections were with two women. Perhaps the strongest connection was with his mother. Even though she did not always approve of his adventuring, Peary wrote home on a regular basis. Much of his correspondence kept his mother up-to-date on his journey toward fame. "Am making myself known," he wrote her once, "and I hope you are satisfied with my progress."[25]

The other woman in his life was his longtime sweetheart, Josephine Diebitsch. The two had met several years earlier at a Washington dance hall and had stayed in touch through Peary's travels. Peary loved Diebitsch very much, but he feared that marriage might mean the end of his dreams of glory. He did not see how he could settle down and marry when he still had places to go and worlds to explore. However, love won out. When he returned from Nicaragua, he and Diebitsch married. They immediately left on their honeymoon, accompanied by his mother.

North Once More

But Peary had not forgotten the Arctic. He believed that the polar regions would bring him the fame he so desperately sought. "I consider it a matter of importance not to let myself drop out of sight,"[26] he wrote his mother in 1890. He took care of his naval duties and seemed to enjoy married life; still, he hoped for another chance to explore. In 1891, he took another leave of absence and began to plan an expedition to northwestern Greenland.

This was an unusual expedition. Peary hired five assistants, among them American doctor Frederick Cook, Norwegian explorer Eivend Astrup, and an African American assistant named Matthew Henson. He also brought along his wife, a decision which shocked many of their friends but on which both Robert and Josephine Peary agreed. Not only was Josephine eager for the adventure, but they both found it a good compromise: This way, he could explore and the two would not be apart. Josephine Peary would be the first white woman to spend a winter so far north.

The party spent their first fall and winter among the Inuit near present-day Thule. Peary reasoned that the Inuit knew the cold and ice far better than any white men of the time. Thus, much of

Peary and his wife Josephine aboard a ship. Mrs. Peary accompanied her husband on several voyages, shocking their friends.

that time was spent learning from the local people. In particular, Peary studied the Inuit system of hauling equipment on sledges—long, low sleds with runners—and using dogs to pull them along. Peary also experimented with different kinds of equipment. "Lightness and strength were the two prime factors," Peary later wrote. "For every ounce of weight which could be saved in equipment, an ounce of food could be substituted."[27]

The following spring, the expedition set out to cross Greenland —the ultimate goal of the trip. The trek was a resounding success. Peary and Astrup traveled five hundred miles to what Peary said was the northernmost point on the island. He reported seeing a channel marking the end of the landmass, but later expeditions proved that this channel was illusory. No one knows whether Peary genuinely thought he had seen it or whether he invented it in his desire to be the first to reach the tip of Greenland. In any case, Peary's journey was remarkable for its speed and its success. "With this one feat," writes a historian, "Peary had vaulted into the ranks of the world's leading explorers."[28]

Another Trip

In 1893, Peary sailed again for Greenland. And again he brought his wife, who was now pregnant. That September she gave birth to a girl, Marie Ahnighito Peary, who later became famous as the "Snowbaby" in a children's book written about her. The following March, Peary set out on another journey across the Greenland ice cap. This was a complete failure; despite being equipped with sledges and dogs, Peary traversed just over one hundred miles before being forced to turn around.

But Peary did not admit defeat. He resolved to send his wife and baby back to the United States without him, while he, Henson, and an American named Hugh Lee spent another winter in Greenland. It was not an easy choice. "The winter has been a nightmare for me," he wrote his wife after his departure. "The only bright moments have been when I was thinking of you."[29] Still, Arctic exploration—and a possible route to the North Pole—took precedence over family.

In April 1895, Peary tried again. This time, the three men traveled more than five hundred miles under terrible conditions. But Peary was not satisfied. His deeper purpose had been to search for a route to the North Pole, and by now he was convinced that such a route did not lie across Greenland. In his eyes, the trip had been a failure. To avoid returning empty-handed, Peary dug up two iron meteorites and brought them back to the United States, not noticing or caring that these meteorites were sacred to the Inuit—and their main source of metal.

"If It Kills Me!"

Upon arriving home, Peary despaired of ever reaching his goal. He was now forty, and all he had accomplished was finding a route that did not reach the North Pole. "I shall never see the North Pole unless someone brings it here,"[30] he told reporters. His wife encouraged him to spend more time at home and give up exploring, but he was not ready to listen. In 1897, Peary pulled some strings to get a five-year leave from the navy.

Peary again sailed north in July 1898, intending an all-out assault on the pole. His route would run between Greenland and Ellesmere Island and continue north. Peary was distressed to learn, however, that Norwegian explorer Otto Sverdrup was in the same area. Sverdrup said he had no intention of going to the pole—and all evidence suggests he did not—but Peary did not believe him. He saw the Norwegian as a competitor and hurried to claim the choice Fort Conger winter camp before Sverdrup could do so. "I'll get to Conger before Sverdrup if it kills me!"[31] a friend quoted Peary as saying.

Peary did get there first—and the effort did nearly kill him. He forced a miserable journey across the winter ice in darkness and in

Peary, pictured here with several of his sled dogs, is dressed for the harsh climate of the Arctic.

temperatures far below zero. Upon arriving at Fort Conger, Peary was quite sick and in need of medical attention. In particular, most of his toes were so badly frostbitten that they were useless and had to be surgically removed. Still, as Peary said, toes were not so important next to the greater goal of reaching the North Pole.

Tragedy

Peary remained in the area for four years. Even though his toes had been amputated, he was unwilling to give in and go home. Instead, he hobbled along, not allowing pain to interfere with his dreams. Nor did he allow family matters to interfere. His wife wrote that she had given birth to a second daughter, Francine, and remarked in her letter that life was slipping away from both of them. But Peary stayed put. "There is something beyond me," he wrote, "something outside of me, which impels me irresistibly to the work [of exploration]."[32]

Family matters beckoned twice more during the trip. In 1901 he received news of the death of his daughter Francine, who lived only seven months. Josephine Peary and their surviving daughter Marie made a trip to Greenland to see him after this tragedy, and Robert did spend some time with them, but although they begged him to return home, he would not. The situation was the same when he received news that his mother had died. "The loss of mother keeps coming to me,"[33] he wrote in his diary, but he refused to consider going home.

Instead, Peary explored. With Henson and several other companions, Peary reached the top of Ellesmere Island, one of the northernmost points of land on the globe. He explored northern Greenland further, too, and in 1902 he ventured onto the iced-over Arctic Ocean in hopes that it would lead him to the pole. It did not. Ridges of ice blocked the travelers' path. Leads, or stretches of open water, appeared from time to time, creating even more havoc. In the end, Peary was forced to return to camp.

Most other explorers might have been satisfied with the four-year journey, but not Peary. His greatest desires remained unfulfilled. He had failed to reach the North Pole; in fact, he had not even come very close. He also could not say that he had gone farther north than any man ever before. An Italian explorer had

African American Matthew Henson accompanied Peary on his failed attempt to reach the North Pole in 1902.

45

recently set that record, and still held it. Nevertheless, Peary took his failures as new challenges. "Next time I'll smash that all to bits," he said, referring to the farthest-north mark. "Next time!"[34]

"Next Time"

His opportunity came quite soon. Almost before Peary had arrived in New York, he was already making plans to ship out again. These plans were much to the dismay of his family. "I have been looking at your pictures," his daughter Marie wrote him, "and I am sick of looking at them. I want to see my father. I don't want people to think me an orphan."[35] Matters became even more difficult when Peary's son Robert was born in 1903. But Peary did not change his mind.

He left New York for Ellesmere Island in July 1905. The new expedition followed a course similar to his previous journeys. Once again, Peary's achievements were remarkable. He braved storms, bad ice conditions, and open leads. He spent sixty-four consecutive days on the polar ice and explored new stretches of Ellesmere Island. He even came back with a new farthest-north record, having indeed smashed the Italian's mark to bits. But he still had not reached the North Pole.

Moreover, there were some nagging questions about his latest expedition. While no one questioned Peary's overall account of the trip, some details did not ring true. Peary's farthest-north record, for example, raised some eyebrows. Peary had left several companions one morning, heading north with Matthew Henson and a few Inuit; within a week, he claimed, they had arrived at a spot thirty-six miles beyond the old record. To cover such a great distance in the short time available would have required the party to travel at an almost incredible speed over the ice.

Furthermore, Peary said there had been no major obstacles blocking their path. If true, this would have helped explain the speeds. But not many Arctic explorers before or since have encountered such smooth going. There was another area of concern as well: Peary was very vague about the details of this trip, especially the return journey south. In fact, it turned out that he had taken no astronomical observations between his farthest-north point and the Greenland coast.

To some, all this was suspicious. It was especially suspicious that none of Peary's companions on this part of the trip knew how to determine the group's position. Thus, there was no independent verification of Peary's observations. During this time, explorers were usually taken at their word, and Peary's story was widely accepted as the truth. Still, several observers could not help but

Peary pictured aboard ship during his last attempt to reach the North Pole.

wonder whether Peary had exaggerated his accomplishments in his frantic search for fame.

The Last Trip

Peary now staked everything he had on one last expedition. He toured the country tirelessly in search of funds, again leaving his family behind in the process. Various wealthy Americans gave him money, and he also earned cash for advertising different products. The *New York Times* offered him $4,000 for his firsthand account of the expedition—*if* Peary reached the North Pole. In July 1908, Peary's ship departed from New York. That September he reached the northern tip of Ellesmere Island.

The following February, Peary headed north. He had developed a complicated system of relays in which some members of the party would travel only part of the way, carrying supplies; as the supplies were used, they would drop back. Peary himself went last in the procession, partly to keep a watchful eye on the rest of the men and partly to conserve his own energy for the final push to the pole.

This was clearly Peary's last chance. He was fifty-two years old, missing seven toes, and under terrible financial pressures. If he did not attain his goal this time, he would be remembered only as the man who consistently failed to reach the North Pole. Alternatively, and perhaps worse, he would fade into obscurity. Neither fate was acceptable to him.

The going was extremely tough, but the men persevered. Ridges of ice rose up fifty feet above the polar surface. The ice cover drifted to the west, then to the east, making a steady northward course almost impossible. For seven days the men waited for one large lead to close. Peary sent first one group of men back, then another. Supplies dwindled. By the end of March, they were still 150 miles from the pole.

At this point, Peary sent everyone back except himself, Henson, and four Inuit men. The six made a frantic dash north. In just five days, as Peary later reported, they covered the full 150 miles, thirty miles a day. No detours had been necessary. Once again, Peary had been blessed with amazing luck just when he needed it. "The Pole at last!!!" Peary wrote in his journal in an entry dated April 7, 1909. "The prize of 3 centuries, my dream and ambition for 23 years MINE at last."[36]

Controversial Legacy

Or was it? Questions about Peary's achievement began to arise soon after he returned home. With time, the questions have grown more insistent. Again, many experts have wondered about the extraordinary speeds claimed by Peary, the almost complete lack of obstacles, and his certainty that he was following a due northerly route despite taking very few observations. Even Peary's historic journal entry of April 7 looks like an afterthought: It was written on a loose sheet of paper and slid inside the journal at some later point.

Some also find it suspicious that, once again, Peary was the only man on the final dash who could determine the group's position. He had sent all his experienced navigators back to base camp earlier in the journey, including one man who had been promised that he would be part of the final push. Moreover, Peary did not share his observations with Henson or permit him to make his own observations at the Pole. Henson could not calculate a position, but he could read instruments well enough. Several historians have speculated that Peary deliberately eliminated any possibility that another witness could challenge his claims.

If Peary did indeed exaggerate or falsify his records, it is impossible at this point to know exactly what he was thinking. Did he do so deliberately, knowing full well that he was lying but afraid to come back a failure? Several experts have put forward this suggestion. Or was his obsession so strong that he managed to convince himself that he actually did reach the North Pole? Others have argued this instead. Either explanation is conceivable.

Peary (center, with cane) is pictured with the National Geographic Society, which staunchly defended him against attacks by critics.

An example of memorabilia produced to honor Peary and Cook, each of whom claimed to have discovered the North Pole.

On the other hand, Peary had his share of supporters then, and he has them now. The National Geographic Society, one of his expedition's chief backers, defended him from critics early on. More recently, the society published an article analyzing the photographs Peary took on his way to and from the North Pole. The author concluded that Peary was where he said he was.

Other supporters have argued that the speeds and sledging conditions claimed by Peary were not out of the question. Indeed, several explorers have had bursts of speed similar to Peary's. And some have experienced surprisingly smooth ice conditions over the Arctic Ocean, especially as they approached the pole. Nevertheless, the controversy continues.

Peary returned home from his final expedition to shocking news: His old companion Frederick Cook had arrived earlier from an Arctic expedition of his own and was claiming that he had beaten Peary to the North Pole. Peary was furious and set about disputing Cook's claim. He was right to do so: Cook's evidence for such a trip was scanty indeed, and most observers today agree that he had not even ventured within several hundred miles of the pole. However, Peary's attacks made him seem mean-spirited. They also inadvertently played up the problems with Peary's own evidence.

After disposing of Cook, Peary settled down to a life of relative ease. Between expeditions, he had lived in Washington. Now he spent summers on Eagle Island, Maine, with his wife and two surviving children. He enjoyed the role of veteran explorer. His advice on overcoming adversity was sought by budding young adventurers and corporate executives alike, and he devoted time to writing about his experiences. He also dabbled in politics and became interested in the then-new science of airplane flight.

Peary could have been satisfied and proud of himself. Whether he had reached the pole or not, he had a long list of accomplishments. He had helped revolutionize Arctic travel; he had explored thousands of square miles of unknown territory; he had shown remarkable courage and leadership. When he died in 1920, he was widely remembered as one of the greatest explorers in history.

Unfortunately, being among the greatest was not enough. Peary had longed for fame, and he had gotten it, but Cook's claims and the questions about his own work mired him in controversy. The fact that some knowledgeable people distrusted his word wounded him. Through books, speeches, and newspaper interviews, he spent his last years trying to eradicate the doubts, but he was never able to lay them completely to rest. Peary's last years were not happy ones, and perhaps it was no wonder. He had set the goal of finding the North Pole above everything else, and in the end that goal consumed him so that nothing else mattered.

CHAPTER 4

Matthew Henson

Among polar explorers through history, Matthew Henson stands out for several reasons. Perhaps most obvious, he was an African American in a field dominated by white Americans and Europeans. Moreover, he never commanded his own expedition, serving instead as Robert Peary's assistant through most of Peary's Arctic career. And Henson remains one of the few explorers to have become more famous after his death than during his lifetime.

But Henson is perhaps most notable for his quick mind and willingness to learn from others. More than most other explorers, he had an eagerness to soak up practical knowledge and information from any source he could find. From early on, he strove to educate himself and to take advantage of opportunities to learn. In particular, Henson was one of the few early explorers who appreciated the culture of native Arctic peoples. Whereas many of his contemporaries dismissed the Inuit as primitive and backward, he learned what he could from the men and women he met on his travels. His expeditions benefited greatly from that decision.

From Cabin Boy to Sailor

Matthew Henson's earliest years gave little indication that he would ever venture toward the North Pole. Unlike many other polar explorers, he did not come from a naval background or a seafaring family. Nor did he grow up in far northern climates. Born in Charles County, Maryland, on August 8, 1866, Henson was the son of poor farmers. When he was four, his family moved to nearby Washington, D.C.

Unfortunately, Henson's mother died several years later. The death changed Henson's family life considerably, and at age thirteen he left Washington to find work. That was not unusual for the time and place: The children of the poor usually did not continue their schooling much beyond that age, if indeed they continued that far. Henson already had a career choice in mind. For several years he had been intrigued by stories of sea adventure. He had also met and talked with some men who worked on Po-

An artist's rendering of a group of Inuit. Matthew Henson was one of the few early explorers who respected the culture of native Arctic peoples.

tomac River steamboats. Hoping for a life on the oceans, Henson walked to Baltimore and headed directly for the city's port.

Henson was young, but he was determined to learn everything he could about ships and sailing. At the harbor he met a veteran sea captain who offered him a chance to serve aboard his merchant ship as a cabin boy. Henson knew that the position of cabin boy was little more than a glorified servant. He would work long hours for low pay; of all the sailors on board the ship, he would rank at the very bottom. Nevertheless, he jumped at the opportunity. In his eyes, the chance to be a cabin boy would help him fulfill his dream.

It quickly became evident to Captain Childs that Henson was a cut above most other cabin boys. Henson had a quick mind and a willingness to work, and his enthusiasm to learn was second to none. Childs took a keen interest in Henson. Over the next several years, as the ship traveled to ports in Russia, China, North Africa, and elsewhere, he instructed Henson in seamanship. The young man quickly attained the status of able-bodied seaman—the position held by most sailors who were not officers.

Childs taught Henson more than typical sailor skills. Noticing Henson's intelligence, he also took the time to continue Henson's education in other ways. In addition to teaching him a little about navigation, he gave the young man lessons in geography, religion, history, and mathematics. Childs also encouraged Henson to learn foreign languages. On an oceangoing ship there was plenty of opportunity for Henson to hear and practice speaking languages other than English. All of these skills helped develop Henson's confidence. They also prepared him for life in the wider world.

In particular, Childs knew that these skills might help Henson combat the prejudice he was likely to encounter. But while racism against African Americans existed everywhere in America, it was perhaps less onerous at sea than it was elsewhere during the late nineteenth century. "I took you aboard 'cause I wanted to give you a chance at life," an early Henson biographer quoted Childs as saying. "How far do you think you'd [have] gotten drifting around on land? You're colored, Matthew, that's a fact and God's wish, but you're a hell of a sight blacker on shore than you are on *my* ship."[37]

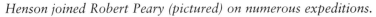

Henson joined Robert Peary (pictured) on numerous expeditions.

When Henson was eighteen, Childs died. At this point, Henson decided not to continue as a sailor. Instead, he traveled up and down the East Coast of the United States, working at a succession of different jobs. Finally, in 1886, he came back to Washington. He moved in with one of his sisters and looked for more permanent work. Before long, Henson was hired by a furrier, a dealer in animal furs. He kept track of the inventory in the company's warehouse and also took on some responsibility for sales, which brought him into contact with customers.

Nicaragua

Among these customers was the explorer and naval officer Robert Peary. Peary had returned to Washington in 1886 after his first trip to Greenland, and he had brought with him a number of furs from Arctic animals. Over the next two years he occasionally brought furs to the store and offered them for sale. During the transactions, Henson and Peary struck up conversations and discovered a mutual interest in travel and exploration.

In 1888, Peary received word that he was being sent to Nicaragua, where the navy expected him to work on plans for a shipping canal. Peary decided that he would need an assistant, and thought Henson would be a likely candidate. Henson did not hesitate to accept the offer. "I recognized in [Peary] the qualities that made me willing to engage myself in his service,"[38] he wrote years afterward. When Peary left for Central America, Henson was at his side.

Officially, Henson was in Nicaragua as Peary's personal servant. In practice, however, he did much more than the job title implied. By all accounts, Henson distinguished himself in Nicaragua just as he had done earlier on board Captain Childs's ship. He had developed strong skills in carpentry and in mechanics, both of which proved useful when dealing with machinery and construction. Peary praised Henson for his "intelligence, faithfulness, and better than average pluck and endurance."[39]

When Peary's stint in Nicaragua was over, Henson left as well. The alliance had been productive for both men. Upon returning to Washington, Henson searched for employment. He eventually resumed his former work at the furrier, but the job did not satisfy him, and he wrote to Peary offering his services again. "If you want me to go back with you to Nicaragua," he said in the letter, "I will be pleased to go with you indeed sir."[40]

In fact, Peary had no plans to return to Central America. But in early 1889, he was reassigned to a Philadelphia naval yard and invited Henson to accompany him there. Again, Henson accepted the offer. He began work as a messenger soon after. As far as Henson was concerned, Peary was simply being a good friend, willing to use his position and influence within the navy to help Henson earn a living. However, Peary was thinking further down the road than Henson knew. Peary was already planning a return trip to Greenland, and he thought the young man might prove useful in this adventure.

Eva Flint

As always, Henson worked hard in his new job. He also began to make the acquaintance of some of the most influential people in Philadelphia's large African American community. In the fall of 1890, he met Eva Flint, a salesclerk in a Philadelphia store whose family was well known and respected in the city. They dated for several months. Henson met her parents and brothers, all of whom approved of him, and the couple began to discuss marriage.

Although he loved Flint very much, Henson had two significant reservations about marrying her. One was financial. He did not believe that he had saved enough money to support a wife yet. Moreover, Henson knew that Flint was an enthusiastic consumer with a particular taste for fine clothing, and he worried that he would not be able to support her in the style to which she was accustomed.

The other reservation had to do with Henson's own suitability for marriage. His enthusiasm for adventure was still very much present. Some of his best memories involved travel—cruising the world as a teenager with Captain Childs, journeying with Peary to Nicaragua. Henson wondered whether he was truly ready to give up these experiences and settle down. Likewise, he wondered whether it would be fair to his wife if he married and then continued to explore, should the opportunity arise.

In February 1891, Henson received a letter from Peary. In it, Peary explained that he would indeed be returning to Greenland, and he invited Henson to go with him. Flint tried to talk him out of it. She noted that he would have to give up his job at the naval yard if he went, with no guarantee of future employment. She also pointed out that Peary could not possibly match the wages paid by the navy.

But Henson knew that there were several potential advantages to going. Any discoveries the two men made would earn Henson personal fame, raising his own status within the black community. His achievements would also reflect positively on African Americans in general. Moreover, Henson argued, this would probably not be Peary's last assignment. If Henson went, Peary might take care of him in the future by helping him find better jobs than the one he presently held.

In the end, Henson could not turn Peary down. The lure of Arctic adventure was too strong. Flint gave in, on the condition that the wedding take place before he left. In April 1891, against the advice of Flint's family, the two married. Two months later, Henson left for Greenland aboard the *Kite*.

The Arctic

As in Nicaragua, Henson was technically Peary's personal servant. But as before, in reality Henson was a full-fledged member of the expedition, and his skills were undeniably useful. He probably had more experience as a sailor than anyone else on the journey, including Peary himself. Once in Greenland, Henson used his carpentry skills to fashion a two-room headquarters for the explorers.

Henson is pictured here leaning against a dog sledge on Robert Peary's ship.

He quickly impressed fellow members of the expedition with his willingness to work and his intelligence.

For the most part, Henson made friends easily among his companions. On his birthday, Peary and his wife threw a party on his behalf. "Never before in my life had the anniversary of my birth been celebrated," Henson wrote many years later, "and to have a party given in my honor touched me deeply."[41] However, Henson did have some difficulties with other members of the expedition. Few—perhaps none—considered Henson truly an equal. "When Henson asserted . . . that black Americans should have the right to vote, for example," writes a historian, "they were quick to remind him of his proper 'place.'"[42]

In particular, Henson repeatedly clashed with a man named John Verhoeff. Verhoeff was not a favorite of Peary's, and he took out much of his resentment on Henson. On one occasion, Verhoeff attacked Henson simply for resting his foot on a table. Verhoeff did not survive the expedition—he lost his footing on a glacier and fell to his death—and after that Henson did his best to downplay the tension that had sprung up between them. Verhoeff and another man who died on a later trip "were good friends of mine," he wrote in his autobiography, "and I respect and venerate their memories."[43]

During the first few months of the expedition, Henson also spent a great deal of time among the local Inuit. Peary approved of this decision, but most other members of the expedition ridiculed Henson's interest. As a rule, earlier explorers had taken little interest in the native people of the Arctic. The Inuit were technologically backward, most adventurers agreed, and they lacked the drive and know-how of Europeans and American whites. Their culture, their religion, their whole way of life was different, and to these nineteenth-century men, "different" implied "inferior."

Henson, however, was not so sure. He was among the first to see what Roald Amundsen and many other explorers after him would recognize: that the Inuit were not to be dismissed but, rather, appreciated and studied. In Henson's eyes, there was no denying that the Inuit had developed many important survival skills that outsiders would do well to imitate. Clothing, sledging techniques, hunting methods—the Inuit had practiced them all for hundreds of years, and despite the hardships of life in the Arctic, the Inuit clearly thrived in their environment.

It was not necessary to like the Inuit people in order to learn from them. Peary himself saw the value of Inuit ways but never held a very high opinion of the Inuit as a group. For him they were simply a tool, a way of getting information. He did not learn their

Henson recognized that Inuit clothing, hunting methods, and sledging skills were all superb assets in surviving the harsh Arctic climate.

language or develop close personal relationships with them as individuals. Henson, on the other hand, did both. "I have come to love these people," he wrote in his autobiography. "I know every man, woman, and child in their tribe. They are my friends and they regard me as theirs."[44]

Other Expeditions

Over the next two decades, Henson spent most of his time in the Arctic. Peary invited him along on every one of his expeditions, and Henson accepted each offer. In the Arctic, he regularly showed his strength and courage. He made nearly every march at Peary's side, sometimes outdistancing his mentor and generally surpassing the efforts of other expedition members. Henson's expertise in Arctic living came in handy again and again. By the time of his second voyage, he was already an experienced sledger, a capable and veteran polar traveler.

Peary generally treated Henson well. Still, he was a man of his time, and in the early 1900s racial prejudice ran rampant. Peary paid Henson less than he paid white men, and in several other ways kept Henson aware of his second-class status. "You have been in my service long enough to show me respect in small things," Peary wrote Henson on one occasion. "[I] have a right to expect you will say sir to me always."[45] Another time, when asked why he had not sent Henson on a journey alone across the Arctic ice pack, Peary explained that the reason was Henson's race. African Americans, he said, lacked the daring and initiative of whites.

Nevertheless, Henson had relatively few complaints. Racism was more significant back home than in the Arctic, so he continued to go north when the opportunity arose. At home, too, Henson was rarely far from Peary's side. In order to stage the expeditions, Peary needed to raise money. He did so in part by giving talks on the Arctic and charging admission. Henson usually came along, often wearing Inuit-style clothing. These lecture tours were exhausting; they took Henson and Peary across most of the United States, and the men often spoke in public more than once a day.

The lecture tour was not the worst, however. Peary also wrote a

Henson adopted the Inuit protective clothing.

one-man show, a play called *Under the Polar Star,* as another fund-raising tool. He assigned Henson to perform it as part of a separate tour. The effort nearly did Henson in. "Mr. Peary," he wrote in an 1896 letter, "I don't think that I could stand going around this winter. I have been sick ever since I have been in Chicago and now I am hardly able to get to the theater—but I have to do it, or walk home."[46]

At times, Henson considered giving it all up and returning home to Philadelphia, a city he now seldom visited. The physical labors of exploration took their toll, as did the constant Arctic cold. "When I left for home and God's Country [the United States] the following September," Henson said about the end of one expedition, "it was with the strongest resolution to never again! no more! forever! leave my happy home in warmer lands."[47] But he changed his mind. Just as Peary was determined to reach the North Pole, so too was Henson.

The constant travel had an effect on Henson's marriage as well. Eva Flint Henson resented the amount of time her husband spent away from her. In 1896, tensions between the Hensons grew so high that Eva wrote to Peary to ask about his plans. "I hear you are going to Greenland again," she said. "Will you please inform me when you expect to go and how long you are going to stay . . . as Matt says he is going with you."[48] The relationship did not last. The couple divorced in 1897.

Toward the Pole

Henson and Peary traveled extensively through Greenland and the Canadian Arctic during their voyages. In between expeditions, they lectured; in between lecture tours, Henson took on several odd jobs such as serving as a building janitor and a railroad porter. In each case, though, he was simply biding his time until the next expedition.

By 1908, Henson had undertaken six expeditions in all. Each had brought back new geographic information, and some had been of scientific interest as well. But the two men had not attained their greatest goal: finding the North Pole. In 1908, soon after Henson married Lucy Ross, the daughter of his landlady, they left New York to try again.

Although Henson was in his early forties by the time he and Peary embarked on their last expedition, he did not believe that he was too old to reach the pole. Indeed, Henson had extensive experience in nearly all aspects of exploration. The one exception was navigation, of which Captain Childs had taught him only the basics. "I hope to perfect myself in navigation," Henson wrote as the ship departed the United States. "I need to master the mathematical end."[49] He could use tools to make astronomical observations, in other words, but he could not do the calculations necessary to establish his position.

Henson did study a little navigation at winter camp, but he was too busy with other tasks to learn much more than he already knew. He soldered closed cans of fuel, took care of the sled dogs, and constructed many of the expedition's sledges. Once the expedition began its northward push to the pole, Henson was one of the men who helped create a trail. With a team of Inuit, he chopped through ice ridges, figured out the best way around thin ice, and constructed snow houses along the path.

Traveling required Henson's carpentry and mechanical expertise, too. At one point, a team member lost control of a sledge atop a thirty-foot-high wall of ice. The sledge crashed to the bottom of the ridge, breaking in two. Henson was able to repair the sledge with strips of seal hide. On another occasion, the men ventured across an unstable sheet of ice. Wave action beneath the sheet pushed three sledges against the side of an ice floe, damaging all three. Working quickly, Henson constructed two new sledges from the pieces he could salvage.

Peary's system of relays and support parties required that men turn back from time to time. Henson was desperate to go to the pole, but he knew that Peary alone would decide who would be in the final push. The uncertainty caused him great anxiety. On March 25, 1909, with a group of explorers due to be sent back, Peary summoned Henson for a private talk. Henson approached his leader with great trepidation, but relaxed once Peary assured him that he would still be needed. "My heart stopped palpitating," he remembered afterward, "I breathed easier, and my mind was relieved. It was not my turn yet, I was to continue onward."[50] Indeed, Henson—along with four Inuit—would continue onward all the way to the pole.

The last five days of the trip to the pole were extremely difficult for Henson. "We marched and marched," he wrote, "falling down in our tracks repeatedly, until it was impossible to go on."[51] At one point, Henson fell into an open stretch of water; fortunately, his Inuit companion Ootah fished him out just before Henson could drown or freeze to death. The physical strain was matched by the mental. Henson did not know how much progress they were making toward the pole. Peary was the only man remaining who could calculate their position, and he chose not to share this information with Henson.

Even when the journey came to an end, Peary at first kept quiet about it. He called a halt and traveled a little farther on while Henson and two of the Inuit prepared the camp. When Peary returned, he took several observations but still remained silent. Henson guessed that they were now at the pole itself. As he wrote later,

> I was confident that the journey had ended. Feeling that the time had come, I ungloved my right hand and went forward to congratulate [Peary] on the success of our eighteen years of effort, but a gust of wind blew something into his eye, or else the burning pain caused by his prolonged look at the reflection . . . of the sun forced him to turn aside.[52]

Whatever the reason, Peary did not shake Henson's hand. Instead, he went into his tent to sleep. The next morning, he finally confirmed that they were at the pole.

The trip back, as Henson described it, was difficult as well. Peary had become completely exhausted and spent much of the trek resting on the sledges. "He was practically a dead weight,"[53] Henson admitted. Perhaps worse, Peary was almost completely silent, refusing to speak to Henson if he could avoid it. Henson did not understand his leader's behavior and was deeply hurt by it, but Peary either did not notice or chose not to apologize.

Returning Home

When the expedition returned

Henson onboard ship following the Peary expedition's return to the United States.

to the United States, most public attention for the feat was directed at Peary alone. For example, Peary received a medal from the National Geographic Society; Henson did not. Henson was overlooked partly for reasons of race but also for reasons of rank. And Peary was not one to share credit with others. Sometimes he was not even one to give credit where it was due. The story of discovery that he told backers and journalists tended to play down the role of Henson and other members of the party while emphasizing his own accomplishments.

By now, Henson was no doubt used to Peary's methods, and he did not let them bother him unduly. He also recognized that his achievement was important for blacks everywhere, even if he himself did not receive much attention for it. Henson consoled himself with the thought that the past was full of people of color doing remarkable things without credit. "As in the past," he remarked, "from the beginning of history, wherever the world's work was done by a white man, he had been accompanied by a colored man."[54] His role in the discovery of the North Pole, he pointed out, simply followed this pattern.

While serving as a customs clerk in New York City, Henson followed the routes of other explorers who reached the North Pole by air.

Henson also did not play much of a part in the controversy that followed the explorers' safe return when several other explorers suggested that the men had fallen far short of the pole. By all evidence, Henson accepted Peary's observations as accurate. However, his accounts of the journey do differ in several ways from Peary's recollections. Henson's descriptions of travel conditions in the far north, in particular, suggest that the expedition moved more slowly than Peary said it did. Whereas Peary reported nothing but smooth surfaces, Henson described open water and high ridges of ice. If Henson's notes were accurate, they tend to support the notion that the six men did not have time to reach the North Pole.

Henson's feat did draw him some attention. He collaborated with a ghostwriter on an autobiography, published in 1912, and was interviewed by several newspapers and magazines. In 1913, in appreciation for his work, President William Howard Taft appointed Henson a customs clerk in New York City, a position he held until he retired in 1936. By then, Peary was long since dead, and Henson had been very nearly forgotten.

In the late 1930s, however, Henson's anonymity began to change. The year after he retired, Henson was given an honorary membership in New York's Explorers Club, an organization dedicated to travel and adventure. The following year, a Danish geologist named a Greenland glacier after him. In 1944, all surviving members of the Peary expedition were awarded a Congressional medal, and in 1948, the Geographic Society of Chicago presented Henson with a gold medal in recognition of his achievements.

Legacy

Henson died in New York City on March 9, 1955. He was eighty-eight years old. Henson and his wife had never had much money; until his retirement, both had worked full-time. Indeed, money was so tight that Lucy had her husband buried in the same plot where her mother's remains had been laid to rest over thirty years before. The couple had no children; like Peary, Henson produced a son with an Inuit woman during his years in Greenland, but he never knew the son and may have been unaware of the boy's existence.

After Henson's death, his star continued to rise. The civil rights movement of the 1960s brought increased public attention to black history and important African Americans through the years. Henson was one of the people whose life and work was rediscovered

At eighty-one, Henson reads from Negro Heroes *magazine. Henson gained recognition and renown late in life.*

during this time. Since then, he has been the subject of many books and articles, and he has been posthumously granted a number of medals and other awards. Will Steger, an explorer who sledged to the North Pole in 1986, even dedicated a book about his experiences to the memory of Henson, calling him "the greatest unsung hero in the history of Arctic exploration."[55]

The attention is well deserved. Henson was not simply an assistant on the Peary voyages, a man who came along for the ride while the real work was done by others. The records show, instead, that he was a valued and critical member of the expeditions. His expertise in mechanics and carpentry came in handy time and again, and his willingness to learn from the Inuit helped immeasurably.

Whether or not Henson and Peary actually made it to the North Pole, Henson deserves to be remembered today. He was a true collaborator on some of the most dramatic and interesting polar voyages ever undertaken. He overcame long odds to reach his goals. And perhaps most important of all, he was a man who never allowed himself to stop learning.

CHAPTER 5

Roald Amundsen

Of all the polar explorers in history, Roald Amundsen is perhaps the greatest. Not only was Amundsen the first man to reach the South Pole—the achievement for which he is best remembered today—but he was also the first to navigate the Northwest Passage. Amundsen also made a journey to the North Pole as well. There were three significant polar destinations during the nineteenth and early twentieth centuries, and Amundsen's name is connected with the exploration of all three.

But Amundsen's greatness comes from more than these achievements. His expeditions were consistently well run and well organized. He knew more about routes, conditions, and equipment than most of his contemporaries, and his range and versatility were second to none. Very few other explorers of his time ventured to both the Arctic and the Antarctic, as Amundsen did. Likewise, Amundsen was unusual in that he was a strong backpacker, an expert sledger, and a capable sailor, allowing him to travel equally well on land, over ice, and across the sea.

Open Windows

Roald Amundsen was born in the small coastal town of Hvisted, Norway, on July 16, 1872. His father was a merchant who owned a shipyard—the sea was an important part of young Roald's life from early on. Even when he and his family moved to Oslo, then called Christiania, the Norwegian capital city, the Amundsens continued to spend as much time as they could in Hvisted.

Amundsen was the youngest of four sons, and he spent much of his childhood trying to keep up with his brothers. The boys quarreled often and sometimes used physical force against each other. Because he was the youngest of the brothers, Roald often received the brunt of teasing and bullying. Perhaps as a result, he worked hard to achieve physical toughness and athleticism.

Amundsen was more than successful. Like many Norwegians, he became an expert skier at an early age. He played soccer to develop his stamina, although he never especially enjoyed the sport,

Roald Amundsen is pictured here beginning a polar trek by dogsled.

and he went for long and arduous hikes through the countryside. Sometimes he went accompanied by his brothers or other friends; sometimes he went alone. When Amundsen was summoned for military duty, the army doctor who examined him excitedly called in the other physicians to marvel at his muscles. "I was terribly embarrassed by this public viewing," Amundsen admitted later. "I wanted the ground to open and swallow me."[56]

His desire for fitness had a purpose beyond mere self-defense. By his early teens, Amundsen had developed a career goal: He wanted to be an Arctic explorer. Books and newspapers about earlier expeditions were readily available in Christiania, and Amundsen took full advantage of them. He read everything he could find that pertained to the polar regions. He spent as much of the wintertime outdoors as he possibly could. He even slept with his bedroom windows wide open during the coldest nights, so that he would be ready for the rigors of the polar climate.

Amundsen's mother, however, took a dim view of her son's interests. Roald's father had died when he was fourteen, and she carried firm authority in the house. She had hoped for academic excellence from all her boys, but only one of the first three had done well in school, and all three had gone off to sea. Roald represented her only remaining hope.

Instead of supporting her son's ambitions, Amundsen's mother sent him to college with the hope that he would become a doctor. Amundsen enrolled in the proper courses, but grudgingly. He seldom studied, devoting most of his energy to researching polar matters instead. He stuck it out, though, until he was twenty-one. That year his mother died, and Amundsen left school for good.

Experience

Amundsen had already begun to draw up a long-range plan for leading his own polar expedition. He had plenty of physical strength and stamina, and he had plenty of book knowledge. Both would prove helpful, but he would need much more. High on his list was actual polar experience, or something very close to it. He

Amundsen using a sextant.

would also need further nautical experience. Amundsen was determined to be the sole commander on any journey he undertook, and that meant learning everything he could about each aspect of the voyage.

His first step was to try skiing in the Norwegian mountain wilderness in conditions similar to what he might encounter in Greenland or Antarctica. In early 1894, Amundsen and two friends undertook a winter journey across the mountains of central Norway, a dangerous area hardly ever visited during the winter. Unfortunately, their jackets and blankets were too heavy, and the skis did not work as planned. In the end, the men were unable to complete their trip.

But Amundsen was far from daunted. As he would throughout his life, he looked at these problems not as insurmountable failures but as opportunities to make improvements. In 1896 he returned to the same area, this time with better skis, better bindings, and lighter jackets. He also brought along three compasses to make sure he did not get lost. The trip was grueling and took him much longer than he expected, but this time he reached his goal.

In between these skiing expeditions, Amundsen signed up to crew on several ships, hoping to earn his skipper's license as well as to gain polar experience. His first berth was on a Norwegian ship called the *Magdalena*. This ship was used for seal hunting, and it crisscrossed the Arctic in search of prey. Amundsen did not especially enjoy the work, but he kept his ears and eyes open and learned about clothing, boatbuilding, and more from the experience.

Amundsen followed this trip with similar voyages, earning his first mate's certificate in 1895. Two years later, still itching with polar fever, he volunteered for duty aboard a ship called the *Belgica*. A former sealing vessel, the *Belgica* now belonged to a Belgian naval officer, Adrien de Gerlache, who was planning a trip to Antarctica. Pleased with Amundsen's experience, de Gerlache hired the Norwegian without hesitation.

The voyage of the *Belgica*, though, was very nearly a disaster. De Gerlache proved to be an incompetent commander. The expedition was badly planned and undersupplied. Disease ran rampant through the crew. The ship was frozen solid within the ice pack, requiring the men to cut an escape channel; it limped to the safety of South America in March 1899.

Most of the men on the journey would never again return to the Antarctic. Amundsen was an exception. Whereas others thought the Antarctic an empty and forbidding place, his experience had been otherwise. He had been captivated, and he intended to return someday. In one writer's words, he "thought the continent a sleeping beauty awaiting her kiss."[57]

The Northwest Passage

For now, however, Amundsen turned his attention to the north. He had enough nautical experience to qualify for a captain's license, and he began to think about making a voyage through the Northwest Passage. His extensive research on the subject, coupled with his skiing and hiking skills and his seamanship, made him an excellent candidate to navigate the passage. There was only one problem—finding financial backers willing to support him in his quest.

The question of finances dogged most polar explorers, but it was of particular concern to Amundsen. Many other voyagers had been naval commanders; Amundsen, however, did not have that built-in source of funds and crew. Other explorers had been backed by business interests, but earlier efforts had demonstrated that the Northwest Passage had no commercial value. Indeed, explorer John Franklin's experience had suggested that it might not be navigable at all.

Amundsen, however, did not let these problems discourage him. In Antarctica, he had been impressed with the knowledge of the scientists who accompanied the expedition. Moreover, he realized that the presence of the scientists had helped encourage wealthy backers to fund de Gerlache's expedition. Amundsen thus resolved to learn what he could about the science of the polar regions, hoping that a scientific purpose could attract money when mere romantic ideals could not.

In particular, Amundsen decided to learn all he could about the North Magnetic Pole, which lay close to his proposed route. The pole had been discovered some time earlier by British explorer James Clark Ross, but much about it remained unknown. No one knew, for instance, if the magnetic pole stayed in the same place all the time or if its exact location shifted from year to year. Showing characteristic zeal and single-mindedness, Amundsen traveled to Germany to study magnetism with an expert on the subject. The professor was delighted when he heard of Amundsen's intentions. "If you [study the magnetic pole]," he told Amundsen, "you will be the benefactor of mankind for ages to come."[58]

Armed with his new expertise, Amundsen headed home to talk to his country's leading explorer, Fridtjof Nansen. Nansen, who had attained celebrity status for his Arctic journeys, promised his full support. Patriotic Norwegians, urged on by Nansen, contributed to Amundsen's venture in hopes that he would bring

Norway fame and glory. The trip, Amundsen soon realized, might become a reality.

The *Gjøa*

Over the next two years, Amundsen planned his journey. He bought a small ship, the *Gjøa*, and took it on several training runs. The ship was tiny compared to those used by Franklin and other earlier explorers, but Amundsen believed it would be perfect for his purposes. Indeed, the *Gjøa* was built to withstand the shocks of floating ice, and it could navigate narrow streams and openings in the ice that a larger ship could never manage.

Amundsen hired six men and pared the supplies down to as little as possible. The expedition, he told friends, would find its own food, construct its own shelters, and rely on itself. That was necessary, for Amundsen knew that the voyage would be long and complicated. In June 1903, he left Norway and made his way through the islands of the Canadian Arctic. By the beginning of winter, the group had reached King William Island in the central Arctic.

There Amundsen stopped. He had promised his backers that his trip would have a scientific component, so the men built an observatory and began searching for the North Magnetic Pole. The ship froze in place, and the men stayed on the island for two full years of observations. Amundsen proved that the magnetic

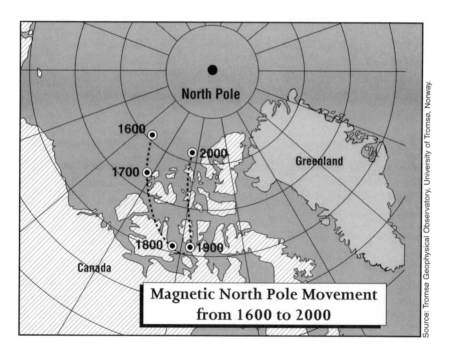

Magnetic North Pole Movement from 1600 to 2000

Source: Tromsø Geophysical Observatory, University of Tromsø, Norway.

pole had shifted about thirty miles since Ross's time. The discovery that the magnetic pole was not fixed ranked as his greatest contribution to science.

Amundsen's group was joined for most of this time by a group of local Inuit, who were intrigued by the Europeans and their activities. Unlike many earlier explorers, Amundsen did not dismiss the Inuit as backward and primitive. Instead, he set out to learn from them. The Inuit taught Amundsen and his men how to dress for the polar conditions, how to paddle a kayak, how to stave off frostbite, and much more. "Now I can move as I want to," Amundsen wrote with delight after trying traditional Inuit clothing for the first time—deerskin parkas and stockings, long, thick gloves that went halfway up the arm, and boots stuffed with absorbent sedge grass. "Am always warm, without sweating."[59]

In early August 1905, the ice broke up around King William Island, and Amundsen and his crew headed west. Their path now led through Simpson Strait, a shallow and narrow waterway typically choked with ice and rocks. No ship before them had managed to traverse the strait. This was the main challenge of Amundsen's route; it was what had prevented any expedition from completing the Northwest Passage before. The journey through the strait was harrowing. But they moved forward steadily and carefully. Before long, they were out of the strait.

The men continued west. At the end of August, they encountered a whale ship from the Pacific. Amundsen was delighted. "The North-West Passage had been accomplished—my dream from childhood," he wrote in his journal. "I suppose it was weakness on my part, but I could feel tears coming to my eyes."[60] Unfortunately, the season was late and the Gjøa was soon locked into ice for a third winter just northeast of Alaska. Amundsen was so eager to tell the world of his achievement that he made a six-week sledge run to the town of Eagle, Alaska, and cabled Nansen the news.

Which Way?

Amundsen returned to the Gjøa the next spring and sailed home to adulation. He met with a number of famous people and was lionized as a great Norwegian; Norway had just gained its independence from nearby Sweden, and he became one of its earliest national heroes. Soon after, he fell in love briefly with an unhappily married woman, Sigrid Castberg, but she refused to leave her husband for him.

Other than that interlude—the only serious romance he ever seems to have had—Amundsen devoted all of his energies to the

Amundsen and his crew pose aboard the ship they navigated through the Northwest Passage.

question of another expedition. Amundsen saw exploration as the most important part of his life. He had no living parents, no family of his own, and no great interests in academia or other professions. Instead, he devoted himself almost entirely to his polar voyages.

He next turned his attention to the still-undiscovered North Pole. Over the next few years, he studied oceanography, again trying to lend a scientific purpose to the romance of finding the pole, and he did his best to raise funds for the journey. He also negotiated for the use of Nansen's ship the *Fram*, which like the *Gjøa* had been built specifically to withstand the pressure of Arctic ice. At last he announced a starting date for his voyage: the early months of 1910.

But several months before Amundsen could leave, Robert Peary announced that he had reached the North Pole. The race to get there first was over. Publicly, Amundsen maintained that Peary's feat did not affect him. He would still head north, he said; there would be important observations and geographic discoveries left to make. Privately, however, Amundsen had different ideas. There would be no glory in reaching the pole after Peary. Thus, he decided he would head not for the North Pole but for the still-undiscovered South Pole.

However, Amundsen kept the news to himself. He postponed the departure of his expedition to July 1910, which gave him time to plan for the different terrain and conditions of Antarctica. In the meantime, he bought dogs, experimented with skis, and pored over maps, all the while pretending that the North Pole was his destination. He continued to fund-raise, too, telling people that his real interest was the scientific work he had planned rather than the honor of discovery.

Amundsen had several reasons for concealing his true intentions. For one, he was by nature secretive and unwilling to share his plans. For another, he suspected that some of his backers might not approve of the idea. Finally, English naval officer Robert Scott was mounting a much more public assault on the South Pole. Scott was scheduled to leave England in August 1910. Amundsen feared giving the patriotic English a reason to overwhelm their countryman with financial and material support.

In the end, Amundsen did not even tell his crew of the change in plan. Except for two ship's officers and a handful of friends, no one knew Amundsen's secret when they left Norway. The other crewmen did not find out the truth until September, when the *Fram* arrived at the Atlantic port of Madeira, a Portuguese possession off the African coast. After informing the crew, Amundsen also wrote letters home to Nansen and other friends not yet in on the secret. Finally, he cabled Robert Scott. The telegram was brief and to the point. "Am going South,"[61] it read.

Antarctica

Amundsen chose as his landing point the Bay of Whales on the Ross Ice Shelf. Sometimes called the Great Ice Barrier, the Ross Ice Shelf was a frozen bay extending up to three hundred miles southward into the Antarctic continent. The Norwegians arrived in January 1911, set up a hut, and began killing enough seals to supply the group with fresh meat through the winter. They also started to place supplies along the route to the pole. The idea was to leave extra food, fuel, and equipment on the way. The more the men could leave, the less they would need to carry to ensure they returned safely.

This process was called "depot laying," and it was the first opportunity Amundsen had to try out his dogs, skis, and equipment

A member of Amundsen's Antarctic expedition team poses with sledge dogs during their journey to the South Pole in 1911.

in true Antarctic conditions. Except for some problems with his boots, he was delighted at the results. During three such journeys, the men succeeded in laying depots almost halfway to the pole. After that, winter set in and the men began preparing their equipment for the push to the pole.

Amundsen knew that Scott had set up a base at the other end of the Ross Shelf. Fearing that his rival might beat him to the South Pole, Amundsen set a very early starting date: the end of August, still technically winter in Antarctica. It was a mistake. The men left as planned, but after four days of extremely bitter temperatures, they returned to base. Amundsen was right to order the return. As it was, several men ended up with frostbite.

On October 20, they tried again. This time the temperatures were more moderate, and the five men on the journey made excellent time. "Dogs as if possessed," marveled one member of the team, "careered off like madmen. Going good and terrain flat and fine."[62] On a typical day, the men traveled for five or six hours and covered nearly twenty miles—a strong pace for polar travel.

By November 4, 1911, they had reached the last depot, less than five hundred miles from their goal.

The remaining distance was great, but Amundsen was confident. He had plenty of food and fuel. Even if he missed some of the depots on the way back, he calculated that he and his men could reach safety without trouble. Still, speed was of the essence. As a result, when Amundsen came to the end of the ice shelf, he headed directly south into the mountains rather than looking for an easy pass.

It was very nearly a fatal mistake. Later explorers proved that there were, in fact, many easier ways into the interior of Antarctica. But Amundsen had made his choice, and he stuck to it. The straight path into the mountains was steep and dangerous. Along the way, the men had to traverse the extremely hazardous Axel Heiberg Glacier, a solid sheet of ice on the side of one of the mountains. But the group was successful. In four days of concentrated effort, they climbed ten thousand feet, bringing with them forty dogs and a ton of supplies—a remarkable feat indeed.

The Final Push

Once Amundsen had reached the top of the mountain range, the hardest part of the trip was over. His careful planning and constant tinkering had paid off. The light sledges kept them traveling at a good pace, and the warm clothing kept them from frostbite. As they traveled, they laid more depots, further lightening the load. With less to pull, fewer dogs were needed, and the men killed about half the remainder. Amundsen did not like the cruelty involved but saw no alternative if he was to reach the pole safely. Not only did fewer dogs require less food, but the carcasses provided fresh meat for the remaining dogs as well as the men.

Still, conditions were far from ideal. "Fog, fog, and again fog," wrote Amundsen. "Also fine falling snow, which makes the going impossible."[63] The men had to contend with several blizzards as well. Worse was a sheet of slow-moving ice riddled with dangerous holes called crevasses. The group spent four days maneuvering through its hazards; a single misstep would have meant death. Once, one man's sledge ran out partly across an empty yawning pit. Several dogs dangled helplessly from their traces before the men could pull them back.

From there, however, the travel was smooth. The men soon reached the polar plateau, a high, flat land surrounding the South Pole. The question now was not whether the Norwegians would reach the pole but whether they would get there first. They were

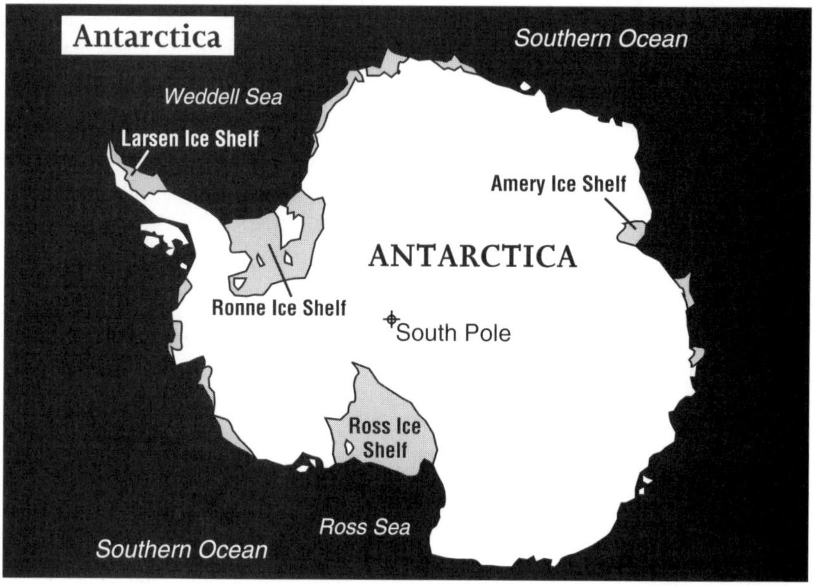
Antarctica
Southern Ocean
Weddell Sea
Larsen Ice Shelf
Amery Ice Shelf
ANTARCTICA
Ronne Ice Shelf
South Pole
Ross Ice Shelf
Ross Sea
Southern Ocean

in luck: On December 15, when they reached their destination, there was no sign of Scott. "So we arrived," Amundsen wrote in his journal, "and were able to plant our flag at the geographical South Pole. God be thanked!"[64]

But the Norwegians were not through yet. They were determined that no one be able to question their achievement as some scientists and explorers had questioned Robert Peary's claim of reaching the North Pole. To be safe, Amundsen and his men traveled in a so-called box around the area, covering a square of several miles on a side; that way, if their original observations had been slightly off, the pole would still be within their route.

Knowing that Peary's observations had been called into question, the men also checked and double-checked their figures and continued to make observations for a full twenty-four hours after arrival. Finally, they set up a tent with discarded equipment and a letter to the Norwegian king. The materials would stay put, proof to later adventurers that Amundsen and his party had reached their destination.

New Plans?

The trip back was far from easy. The men got lost several times and had trouble finding several of their depots. The high altitude of the mountains made breathing difficult, and descending the glaciers at the edge of the ice shelf was no easier than climbing them had been. And, of course, the men were weary from the physical and mental demands of several weeks on the trail. But on January 26, 1912, the men returned safely to the Bay of Whales.

The expedition had been a tremendous success. Amundsen had planned exceptionally well, meeting every challenge with care and forethought. There were no deaths or serious injuries on the way to or from the pole. The explorers never ran low on food or shelter, either. The trip was so successful, in fact, that Amundsen feared their story was too dull. "We haven't got much to tell in the way of privation or great struggle," Amundsen remarked the day after they arrived. "The whole thing went like a dream."[65]

The men packed up their base camp and the *Fram* returned to civilization, where Amundsen announced his news. Most Norwegians were proud of their countryman's achievement. Much of the rest of the world agreed. But many English were angry. They saw the South Pole as Scott's to discover, and they were furious at Amundsen's deception in traveling south when he had announced plans to head north.

The Amundsen expedition at base camp en route to the South Pole.

Amundsen seemingly paid little attention to his critics. He embarked on a lecture tour and began planning another Arctic expedition. He hoped to sail into the pack ice, as Nansen had done, and drift over the North Pole itself. However, he soon gave up on this idea. Nansen had done it so well that Amundsen's proposed voyage could not add much that would be new.

Slowly, Amundsen began to realize that his discovery of the South Pole was, in an odd way, a curse. He could never hope to duplicate the excitement or the glory of that time. The realization discouraged him. "He seemed distinguished," wrote an acquaintance during this time, "but somehow a little decayed."[66] Worse, since he had never had much of a personal life, he had nothing else to fall back on. So much of his energy had been devoted to exploration, and now he had evidently run out of worlds to explore.

For several years, Amundsen tried to concentrate on other projects. He went into the shipping business and learned to fly airplanes. In 1918, however, he returned to the Arctic. He bought a ship called the *Maud* and sailed it along the northern coast of Siberia. The ship did drift partway across the Arctic Ocean, and became just the second ship to travel along the Northeast Passage over the top of Europe and Asia. However, being second was not enough for Amundsen.

To the Skies

Finally, Amundsen had a brilliant new idea: He would become the first man to fly across the Arctic Ocean. A wealthy American, Lincoln Ellsworth, offered to sponsor his attempt. In 1925, with Amundsen now well into his fifties, he and Ellsworth headed north in two small planes. They made it as far as the eighty-eighth parallel, where conditions forced them to land. One of the vehicles was damaged beyond repair in the landing, and Amundsen and Ellsworth barely managed to return to civilization with the other.

A year later, Amundsen tried again, this time with an Italian named Umberto Nobile as his partner. The two flew from the Norwegian island of Spitsbergen, passed over the pole itself, and landed safely in Alaska. The trip took two full days. Amundsen could now be remembered not only as a great sledger, sailor, and skier, but also as a pilot. He would also go into history as the first man to reach both the North and South Poles.

Following his achievement, Amundsen devoted himself to wrapping up his career as an explorer. He did his best to pay off old financial debts, which were many; never a very good fund-raiser, he had often left on expeditions just before his creditors could catch

Amundsen (pictured) was determined to find his polar flying partner Umberto Nobile, who had vanished on a subsequent flight to the North Pole.

up with him. In 1927, he published his memoirs. The book showed that he had indeed been stung by the criticisms directed toward his South Pole work. In particular, he was angry at the English, who he felt had never given him his proper due as an explorer.

In 1928, Amundsen returned to the Arctic for the last time. Nobile, his partner on the transpolar flight, had disappeared on another flight to the North Pole. Amundsen expected to be put in command of the rescue operations. "I'm ready to go right away,"[67] he told friends as soon as he heard the news. When he was not chosen to lead the search, he did not wallow in disappointment. Instead, he decided to mount his own expedition to bring Nobile to safety.

That June, flying an old French plane donated by an admirer, Amundsen left northern Norway for the Arctic. To some observers, the plane seemed too dilapidated to make the trek, but Amundsen was not to be dissuaded. By this time, Nobile had been located by radio. He was somewhere to the north of Spitsbergen; all that remained was to reach him by air and fly him back to Europe. Amundsen was determined to be the man who saved Nobile.

It was the last time anyone would see Amundsen alive. The wreckage of his plane appeared in the Arctic Ocean several months later. It was a tragic end to the life of a great explorer, and yet Amundsen could not have been too disappointed. Just a few days before his death, an Italian journalist had interviewed him and asked him about the lure of the Arctic. "If only you knew how splendid it is up there," Amundsen told the man. "That's where I want to die."[68] In the end, Amundsen got his wish. He finished his life in the place where he had been the most alive and the most content—in the chill, emptiness, and splendor of the Arctic.

CHAPTER 6

Robert Falcon Scott

Most polar explorers gained fame through their successes, but success is not the only possible route to fame. The story of Robert Scott is an excellent case in point. A British naval officer who set out to discover the South Pole, Scott was not especially well prepared for polar conditions. Moreover, while Scott had good points as a leader and an explorer, he could also be stubborn and unrealistic. During Scott's second expedition to the Antarctic, these flaws led him to disaster.

Yet despite that disaster, Scott is better known today than many other more successful polar explorers. His failure could have been dismissed as the result of his own incompetence, but instead it came to be seen as heroic and glorious. In the public eye, Scott seemed different from other explorers: His ideals seemed somehow more noble and pure than Robert Peary's or Roald Amundsen's, and the tragedy of his last expedition was soon viewed as a natural consequence of following those ideals. As a result, even in failure Scott earned fame and stature as an explorer.

Early Years

Robert Falcon Scott was born on June 6, 1868, in Devon, England. His family was well off; his father was a successful businessman, and Robert grew up on a small estate near Plymouth. As a young boy, Robert was often described as shy, quiet, and dreamy. He often fainted at the sight of blood, and he was deeply concerned about the sufferings of animals. Unfortunately, English society did not look upon these characteristics with much tolerance. Men of the time were expected to have strong stomachs and few emotions. Robert worked hard to remedy these perceived flaws.

In addition to a business background, Robert's family came from a strong seafaring tradition. One of his uncles was a naval officer, another a naval surgeon. In 1881, when he was thirteen, Robert followed in their footsteps and joined the Royal Navy as a cadet, the lowest rank among sailors. He did well in training, although the life was rigorous. In 1883, he was promoted to the rank of midshipman, a minor officer, and was sent to join the crew of the naval vessel *Boadicea*.

Over the next few years, Scott served on several ships to general approval. The commander of the *Boadicea*, for example, reported that Scott had served him "with sobriety and to my entire satisfaction."[69] He earned a commission as a sublieutenant in 1888 and another as full lieutenant a year later. His future seemed bright.

In 1894, however, disaster struck his family. His father, now retired, had made some questionable investments and much of the family money had been lost. Although Scott earned a meager salary at best, he and his older brother were forced to help his parents and sisters financially. Three years later, the situation worsened when his father died. At this point, Scott began sending nearly a

English explorer Robert Scott is pictured here as an officer in the Royal Navy.

quarter of his earnings home. If he complained, there is no record of it. Supporting his family was his duty, and Scott accepted it.

Clements Markham

But soon Scott's fortunes changed dramatically. As a midshipman, his abilities and enthusiasm had come to the attention of Clements Markham, a retired naval officer with a strong interest in exploration. Markham was interested in launching a national expedition to Antarctica. He hoped to lay a British claim to the continent; he also hoped to send scientists to study rocks, temperatures, the depth of the ice cap, and much more.

By the summer of 1899, Markham had promises of government support for his venture. All he needed now was an expedition leader. He had a clear idea of the kind of man he sought. As he explained once,

> He must be a naval officer, he must be in the regular line and not in the surveying branch, and he must be young. These are essentials. Such a Commander should be a good sailor with some experience of ships under sail . . . calm yet quick and decisive in action, a man of resource, tactful and sympathetic.[70]

That summer, Scott's path crossed Markham's again. Learning of Markham's search for a leader and realizing that he fit the description perfectly, Scott applied for the post. The fact that he had no previous experience or interest in the polar regions did not seem to matter. Overcoming objections from others who questioned Scott's youth and lack of scientific credentials, Markham officially appointed Scott commander in June 1900, a year before the expedition was to leave.

Scott set to work right away. He took courses in science, gathered supplies, and helped choose the crew. This list included a physician named Edward Wilson and a naval petty officer, Edgar Evans, both of whom would also accompany Scott on his second voyage. It also included another young man, Ernest Shackleton, who would go on to become a famous polar explorer in his own right.

Voyage of the Discovery

Scott and his party left England on July 31, 1901, aboard the *Discovery*, a wooden ship specially built for the rigors of the pounding ice. Unfortunately, the ship was not built for speed, and its progress was slowed still further when it sprang several leaks. In early January 1902, it finally arrived at the Ross Ice Shelf. Over

After a perilous voyage, Scott and his party arrived at the Ross Ice Shelf (pictured).

the next few weeks, Scott made several landfalls and explored about five hundred miles of Antarctic coastline. Since the Antarctic summer is short, however, he soon was forced to set up winter quarters at McMurdo Sound, which lay at one end of the ice shelf.

The first fall and winter were extremely hard on Scott and his men. Conditions were much worse than they had expected. Scott had chosen only a handful of crewmen with polar experience, and the omission showed. The men did not understand how suddenly a blizzard could arise or how quickly flesh would freeze in the bitter cold. "Food, clothing, everything was wrong," Scott later admitted. "The whole system was bad."[71]

To Scott's credit, he and his men learned through trial and error how to cope with the unforgiving environment. One man froze to death soon after their arrival, but before long the rest found ways of staving off the dangers of frostbite. Similarly, the crew's first sledging journeys across the ice nearly ended in disaster, but as time went on the men became more experienced. They were never entirely thrilled with the conditions, however. "There's a fascination about it all," wrote Wilson in his diary, "but it can't be considered comfort."[72]

Scott, however, could have done more to prepare for life in Antarctica. In general, Scott had deferred to Clements Markham's own experiences with Arctic exploration some thirty years earlier. Some of Markham's notions were outdated, but Scott adopted them anyway. In particular, Scott accepted Markham's stance against sled dogs, which by 1900 were widely used in polar exploration. In Markham's view, men were better haulers and more reliable. Moreover, he argued, using dogs was cruel.

Norwegian explorer Fridtjof Nansen, among others, disagreed with Markham's perspective. "I find that with dogs it is easier," he remarked, speaking from years of experience hauling sledges both with and without them. "I agree it is cruel to take dogs; but it is also cruel to overload a human being with work."[73] Nansen's view carried no weight with Scott, however. Markham's experience counted for much more; so did Scott's long-standing concern with avoiding cruelty to animals.

Moreover, Scott saw something very bold and grand in the idea of exploring without the use of dogs. "No journey ever made with dogs," he wrote, "can approach the height of that fine conception which is realised when a party of men go forth to face hardships, dangers, and difficulties with their own unaided efforts."[74] He did carry a few dogs to Antarctica, but Scott left no doubt that he would prefer to have humans do the hauling.

Heading South

The centerpiece of Scott's first expedition was a sledging journey into the heart of the continent, taken by Scott, Wilson, and Shackleton. In early November 1902, the three men left base camp with the intention of traveling as far south as possible. While excited at the prospect of venturing into the unknown, the travelers were also nervous. "Nothing awaits one but an icy desert," wrote Wilson shortly before they left, imagining the landscape to the south, "and one literally carries one's little all [that is, everything] on a sledge!"[75]

At first, the men made reasonably good progress. Each held out vague hopes that they might reach the South Pole itself. Unfortunately, as time went on trouble arose. One problem was the dogs. They could not be controlled, probably because Scott was inconsistent in disciplining them. Worse, they also became ill from eating rotted dog food. Many soon began to die, and those that survived were so badly incapacitated that Wilson eventually put them down.

A more serious problem involved their own food. Even after a year in the Antarctic, Scott had not realized how much nourishment

Scott, Wilson, and Shackleton (left to right) rest during their Antarctic expedition.

the men would need to drag heavy sledges, set up tents, and stay warm. Their food supplies began to run low. And Shackleton soon developed scurvy, a potentially fatal disease caused by lack of fresh food. Reluctantly, Scott turned back.

By any standard, the journey had been a success: Scott and his party had traveled 250 miles farther south than anyone before them. Unfortunately, the trek back was miserable. The food supply was low, Shackleton's condition continued to deteriorate, and their faces were blistered raw by the wind and the glare from the sun. They were lucky to make a safe return to base camp in early February.

Scott remained in the Antarctic until February 1904, an impressive achievement indeed. Despite several near disasters and Scott's general inexperience with Antarctic travel, he could be proud of his accomplishments. He had kept order, learned much valuable geographic and scientific information, and traveled considerably farther toward the South Pole than had any previous explorer.

A Second Expedition

By the time he returned to England, Scott was famous. He was awarded many prizes and honors, including medals from geographic societies and honorary doctorates from universities; some of his admirers believed he deserved a knighthood. Scott moved to London, where he rented a house. He shared the house with his mother, whom he continued to support, but now that he had a captain's pay, the financial stresses were considerably less harsh.

Scott also enjoyed his forays into London's society. One of his sisters had gone into the theater and later married a member of Britain's Parliament. That family connection introduced him to an interesting mix of politicians, business leaders, and creative artists. He also developed other connections on his own, trading on his new status as polar hero. At a party in 1906, he met a sculptor named Kathleen Bruce. She was flamboyant, forceful, and sophisticated, and she was deeply attracted to Scott despite his rather bland and colorless personality. The couple married in 1908; they had one son, Peter.

Aside from family and social matters, Scott occupied himself by lecturing and writing about his experiences. As a naval officer, too, he needed to return to the sea. Fortunately for him, his polar successes won him a command of his own aboard the battleship *Albemarle*. At first, he stated that he would probably never return to the Antarctic, but he soon changed his mind. It was clear to all

The sophisticated Kathleen Bruce Scott poses with the Scotts' only son, Peter.

who knew him that his heart still lay in the polar regions, and besides there was unfinished business: finding the South Pole.

In early 1907, Scott formally began planning a second voyage. The process was not as easy as he had hoped. The English government was not eager to help out, and private donations came in slowly. Part of the trouble was that Scott had difficulty stating a clear goal for his journey. "The main object of the expedition," he said once, "is to reach the South Pole and secure for The British Empire the honour of this achievement."[76] At other times, however, he stressed the scientific value of the expedition. This ambiguity was confusing to the public.

By 1909, two years after he had announced his plans, Scott at last had the financing he needed. He purchased an old whaleship, the *Terra Nova,* and began forming his crew and finding supplies. Mindful of his struggles with sled dogs earlier, Scott brought fewer this time. Instead, he put his trust in a new invention, one still largely untried—a sledge equipped with an engine, similar to a small snowmobile. He also brought along a number of Siberian ponies. The idea was to use the motorized sledges to haul equipment across the relatively flat ice shelf, then switch to the ponies when the expedition reached the mountains.

Amundsen

The *Terra Nova* left England in June 1910. The voyage was long. The crew made several stops for scientific research and to enable Scott to continue to fund-raise. Along the way, however, Scott received some troubling news: a telegram from Norwegian explorer Roald Amundsen stating that he was traveling to the South Pole himself.

Scott had known that Amundsen was heading out on an expedition, but like nearly everyone else, he thought the Norwegian was aiming for the North Pole. The telegram came as a bitter shock. Amundsen was a very capable explorer, and Scott must have known that he would be a formidable rival indeed. The stakes were high, especially after all of Scott's patriotic talk. "If [Amundsen] gets to the Pole first," wrote Scott's companion Titus Oates, "we shall come home with our tails between our legs and no mistake."[77]

For now, however, there was nothing for Scott to do but reach Antarctica and hope to beat Amundsen to the pole. The group arrived at McMurdo Sound in January 1911 and immediately set up camp a few miles north of their previous one. They would not be able to leave for the pole until after the polar winter, but in the meantime they readied as many food and fuel depots as possible.

Robert Scott's ship the Terra Nova *is photographed in Antarctica in 1910, during his attempt to beat Roald Amundsen's expedition to the South Pole.*

The expedition had a scientific purpose, too, and Scott made sure it was not neglected. That winter, several men under the command of Apsley Cherry-Garrard sledged down the coast to observe emperor penguins; the trip was later immortalized by Cherry-Garrard in a book titled *The Worst Journey in the World.* Other scientists investigated the weather and the magnetic properties of the local rocks. For his part, Scott promised to bring back rock samples from the pole if he should reach it.

Scott's primary interest was the pole, and planning for the expedition took most of his time. He calculated how much food would need to be left at each depot and estimated how much the sledges could carry. He ran experiments with the ponies and the motorized sledges. He even tried constructing snow houses for temporary shelter, though few of his companions took this seriously: "Played at building an igloo—with no success,"[78] wrote Wilson in his diary.

At last, spring was in the air and the preparations were complete. In late October, men began to leave from base camp. Over the next few days, more than a dozen crew members headed south. Only a few of these men were scheduled to travel all the way to the pole; the rest would help lay supply depots and maneuver the sledges up the ice before returning. The night before he left, Scott ran through a mental checklist. As far as he could see, he had left nothing undone.

The Second Attempt

Almost immediately, however, the expedition ran into problems. The motorized sledges broke down not far from base camp, and the expedition lacked the parts or know-how to fix them properly. The ponies gave out, too, forcing the men to pull their own sledges. Skis might have improved their pace, but few of the men were experienced skiers. Instead, they walked. Scott wondered if perhaps he had been unwise to give up on dogs, but it was too late now.

There were other problems, too. High winds and blizzards slowed and occasionally stopped the explorers. Worse, the men began to suffer from coughs and sores that would not heal. And Scott had again underestimated the amount of food he and his companions would need. Before they were halfway to the pole, they had already begun eating some of the supplies earmarked for the return trip. Nevertheless, Scott pressed on. On January 3, Scott chose four men who would continue to the pole: Wilson, Oates, Edgar Evans, and Henry Bowers. The remaining men turned around to lay the last depots and head for base camp.

Scott and his crew knew they had just 169 miles to go. Unfortunately, in the last stretch the going began to get tough once more. The five travelers grew increasingly weary and cold. By now, they could travel more than a few miles only with huge mental and physical effort. Their food supplies were not enough to sustain their health. Still, they persevered. On January 13, they crossed 89 degrees south latitude and began the final leg toward the pole.

"An Awful Place"

But on January 16, Bowers noticed a speck on the horizon in front of them. As they drew nearer, they saw that it was a flag. Dog and sledge tracks were clearly visible in the snow: Amundsen had been

No longer able to rely on their motorized sledges, which had broken down, Scott and his men are forced to pull their own sledges.

there first. Refusing to give up, the men nevertheless pulled their sledges a few more miles that day and the next, arriving at the pole late on the afternoon of January 17.

They were the second group ever to reach the South Pole, but that was not good enough for Scott. As he wrote in his journal,

> The Pole. Yes, but under very different circumstances from those expected. We have had a horrible day. . . . Great God! this is an awful place and terrible enough for us to have laboured to it without the reward of priority. . . . Now for the run home and a desperate struggle. I wonder if we can make it.[79]

Scott was right to be concerned. The men were weak, undernourished, and tired, and now they had suffered a deep psychological blow. Base camp lay eight hundred miles away. Oates and Evans contracted frostbite, Scott bruised a shoulder, Wilson

The Scott expedition makes a heartbreaking discovery, finding the Norwegian flag left by Amundsen, who had reached the South Pole first.

strained a leg. But there was no chance to rest. Their diminished rations meant that reaching the next supply depot was of critical importance. Plus, the sledges still had to be pulled by hand, and they now included thirty pounds of the promised rock samples from the pole itself.

In early February, their progress slowed still further. Soft snow held them back. They lost their route several times and wasted precious hours searching for poorly marked supply depots. Getting up and out in the morning became a major struggle, and the men found themselves unable to travel for a full day without risking complete exhaustion. In addition, Edgar Evans's condition was failing rapidly. Unable to keep up on his own, he soon became a burden to the others. On February 17, he slipped into a coma and died.

The survivors still had several hundred miles to go, and things quickly grew worse. Several depots proved to have less oil than anticipated due to leakage (the oil was needed for warmth as well as fuel for cooking). Strong winds and blizzards kept them from making any progress at all for several days at a time. In the middle of March, Titus Oates's feet became so badly frostbitten that he could not continue. When the others refused to go on without him, he stumbled out of the tent and never returned. According to Scott, Oates told them: "I am just going outside and I may be some time."[80]

The party was now down to three. During the next few days, Scott, Wilson, and Bowers struggled on as best they could, although Scott's feet soon became frostbitten. On March 19, the three men camped eleven miles from the next depot. That night, however, another blizzard descended. For two days, Scott and his companions huddled in their tent. The delay cost them the last of their cooking oil and almost all their remaining food. On the 22nd, Wilson and Bowers decided to try to make a mad dash for the depot in the hope of bringing back supplies. As it turned out, the weather was too bad for them even to make an attempt.

For a week, Scott's diary was silent. His final entry, dated March 29, read as follows:

> Since the 21st we have had a continuous gale from WSW and SW. We had fuel to make two cups of tea apiece and bare food for two days on the 20th. . . . Outside the door of our tent it remains a scene of whirling wind. I do not think we can hope for any better things now. We shall stick it out to the end, but we are getting weaker, of course, and the end cannot be far.
>
> It seems a pity, but I do not think I can write more. For God's sake look after our people.[81]

Aftermath

Winter descended quickly in Antarctica, too quickly for the members of the base camp party to mount a major search for Scott when he and his companions failed to return. The following November, when spring came again, a search party traveled inland. The searchers did not take long to find Scott's tent with the three corpses inside. The tent also contained the men's diaries and a few letters, mostly written by Scott in the waning days of his life.

The sledges were nearby, still bearing the rocks hauled from the South Pole. One member of the expedition said he wished the men had spared themselves the weight; without the rocks, they might have been able to travel faster and with less exertion. But most of his companions were delighted, and they rhapsodized about Scott's commitment to science. It was "magnificent," said Apsley Cherry-Garrard, "that men . . . should go on pulling everything they had died to gain."[82]

Tragically, Robert Falcon Scott (pictured) and his men died in the Antarctic, following their failed attempt to be first to reach the South Pole.

Soon, news of the disaster reached the rest of the world. His wife, Kathleen Scott, had journeyed to New Zealand to meet the explorers in what she had hoped would be a triumphant return. She was, of course, crushed by the news of her husband's death. But she joined Cherry-Garrard in applauding Scott's final days. "They would have got through if they hadn't stood by their sick," she pointed out, perhaps accurately, "and so I am very glad that they did *not* get through."[83]

Back home, a few experts questioned Scott's planning and judgment. They blamed his death on his refusal to use dogs, his underestimation of the food the men would require, and his sloppiness in laying supply depots. By far the larger public reaction, however, echoed that of Cherry-Garrard and Kathleen Scott. People agreed that Robert Scott had acted nobly. He had not given up his goal; he had fought till the bitter end; he had continued to work for science even at the cost of his own life. And many further agreed that Scott's rejection of dogs had been especially noble. As Scott had said earlier, it was in some way more pure for men to endure hardships on their own.

In death, Scott became seen as a hero, a brave officer who had accepted his fate without complaint or dishonor. In the words of a biographer, Scott's life demonstrated that "men can still be found to face hardship and even death in pursuit of an idea, and that their unconquerable wills can carry them through, loyal to the last to the charge they have undertaken."[84] The writer spoke for many, then and now, who found Scott's story uplifting despite—or perhaps because of—his ultimate failure. The adventure ended tragically, to be sure, but as Cherry-Garrard put it, it was "a first-rate tragedy."[85]

NOTES

Chapter 1: The Arctic and the Antarctic

1. Quoted in Paul-Emile Victor, *Man and the Conquest of the Poles*, trans. Scott Sullivan. New York: Simon and Schuster, 1963, p. 67.

2. Quoted in Charles Neider, ed., *Antarctica*. New York: Random House, 1972, p. 36.

3. Quoted in Pierre Berton, *The Arctic Grail: The Quest for the Northwest Passage and the North Pole, 1818–1909*. New York: Viking, 1988, p. 21.

Chapter 2: John Franklin

4. Quoted in Berton, *The Arctic Grail*, p. 64.

5. Quoted in Ann and Myron Sutton, *Journey into Ice*. Chicago: Rand McNally, 1965, p. 61.

6. Quoted in Scott Cookman, *Ice Blink*. New York: John Wiley and Sons, 2000, p. 18.

7. Quoted in Berton, *The Arctic Grail*, p. 67.

8. Quoted in Sutton, *Journey into Ice*, p. 144.

9. Cookman, *Ice Blink*, p. 23.

10. Quoted in Fergus Fleming, *Barrow's Boys*. New York: Atlantic Monthly Press, 1998, p. 157.

11. Quoted in Sutton, *Journey into Ice*, p. 172.

12. Quoted in Berton, *The Arctic Grail*, p. 121.

13. Quoted in Cookman, *Ice Blink*, p. 25.

14. Quoted in Berton, *The Arctic Grail*, p. 141.

15. Quoted in Berton, *The Arctic Grail*, p. 145.

16. Quoted in Cookman, *Ice Blink*, p. 75.

17. Quoted in Berton, *The Arctic Grail*, p. 153.

18. Quoted in Berton, *The Arctic Grail*, p. 334.

Chapter 3: Robert Peary

19. Quoted in Berton, *The Arctic Grail*, p. 514.

20. Quoted in Wally Herbert, *The Noose of Laurels*. New York: Atheneum, 1989, p. 40.

21. Quoted in John Edward Weems, *Peary: The Explorer and the Man*. Boston: Houghton Mifflin, 1967, p. 22.

22. Quoted in Berton, *The Arctic Grail*, p. 513.

23. Quoted in Herbert, *The Noose of Laurels*, p. 51.

24. Quoted in Herbert, *The Noose of Laurels*, p. 53.

25. Quoted in Weems, *Peary*, p. 93.

26. Quoted in Weems, *Peary*, p. 101.

27. Robert Peary, *Northward over the Great Ice*. Vol. 1. New York: Frederick A. Stokes, 1898, p. 277.

28. Berton, *The Arctic Grail*, p. 515.

29. Quoted in Berton, *The Arctic Grail*, p. 518.

30. Quoted in Berton, *The Arctic Grail*, p. 520.

31. Quoted in Herbert, *The Noose of Laurels*, p. 112.

32. Quoted in Weems, *Peary*, p. 184.

33. Quoted in Weems, *Peary*, p. 197.

34. Quoted in Berton, *The Arctic Grail*, p. 530.

35. Quoted in Weems, *Peary*, p. 204.

36. Quoted in Berton, *The Arctic Grail*, p. 581.

Chapter 4: Matthew Henson

37. Quoted in Herbert, *The Noose of Laurels*, p. 67.

38. Matthew Henson, *A Black Explorer at the North Pole*. New York: Walker, 1969, p. 3.

39. Quoted in S. Allen Counter, *North Pole Legacy: Black, White, and Eskimo*. Amherst: University of Massachusetts Press, 1991, p. 53.

40. Quoted in Counter, *North Pole Legacy*, p. 54.

41. Henson, *A Black Explorer at the North Pole*, p. 29.

42. Counter, *North Pole Legacy*, p. 59.

43. Henson, *A Black Explorer at the North Pole*, p. 6.

44. Henson, *A Black Explorer at the North Pole*, p. 7.

45. Quoted in Berton, *The Arctic Grail*, p. 527.

46. Quoted in Counter, *North Pole Legacy*, p. 60.

47. Henson, *A Black Explorer at the North Pole*, p. 10.

48. Quoted in Counter, *North Pole Legacy*, p. 61.

49. Henson, *A Black Explorer at the North Pole*, p. 19.

50. Henson, *A Black Explorer at the North Pole*, p. 113.

51. Henson, *A Black Explorer at the North Pole*, p. 130.

52. Henson, *A Black Explorer at the North Pole*, p. 135.

53. Henson, *A Black Explorer at the North Pole*, p. 140.

54. Henson, *A Black Explorer at the North Pole*, p. 136.

55. Will Steger with Paul Schurke, *North to the Pole*. New York: Random House, 1987, dedication page.

Chapter 5: Roald Amundsen

56. Quoted in Roland Huntford, *The Last Place on Earth*. New York: Atheneum, 1986, p. 56.

57. Alan Gurney, *The Race to the White Continent*. New York: W. W. Norton, 2000, p. 282.

58. Quoted in Berton, *The Arctic Grail*, p. 534.

59. Quoted in Huntford, *The Last Place on Earth*, p. 103.

60. Roald Amundsen, *The North West Passage*, New York: Dutton, 1908. vol. 2, p. 125.

61. Quoted in Martin Lindsay, *The Epic of Captain Scott*. New York: G. P. Putnam's Sons, 1934, p. 39.

62. Quoted in Huntford, *The Last Place on Earth*, p. 399.

63. Roald Amundsen, *The South Pole*, vol. 2. New York: Lee Keedick, 1913, p. 78.

64. Quoted in Huntford, *The Last Place on Earth*, p. 454.

65. Quoted in Huntford, *The Last Place on Earth*, p. 492.

66. Quoted in Huntford, *The Last Place on Earth*, p. 532.

67. Quoted in Victor, *Man and the Conquest of the Poles*, p. 244.

68. Quoted in Huntford, *The Last Place on Earth*, p. 540.

Chapter 6: Robert Falcon Scott

69. Quoted in Diana Preston, *A First Rate Tragedy*. New York: Houghton Mifflin, 1998, p. 23.

70. Quoted in T. H. Baughman, *Pilgrims on the Ice*. Lincoln: University of Nebraska Press, 1999, p. 26.

71. Quoted in Lindsay, *The Epic of Captain Scott*, p. 32.

72. Quoted in Ann Savours, ed., *Edward Wilson: Diary of the Discovery Expedition*. New York: Humanities Press, 1967, p. 130.

73. Quoted in Huntford, *The Last Place on Earth*, p. 137.

74. Quoted in Preston, *A First Rate Tragedy*, p. 5.

75. Quoted in Savours, *Edward Wilson*, p. 209.

76. Quoted in Preston, *A First Rate Tragedy*, p. 101.

77. Quoted in Huntford, *The Last Place on Earth*, p. 304.

78. Quoted in Francis Spufford, *I May Be Some Time: Ice and the English Imagination*. New York: St. Martin's Press, 1997, p. 325.

79. Quoted in Neider, *Antarctica*, p. 228.

80. Quoted in Neider, *Antarctica*, p. 265.

81. Quoted in Neider, *Antarctica*, p. 267.

82. Quoted in Huntford, *The Last Place on Earth*, p. 521.

83. Quoted in Huntford, *The Last Place on Earth*, p. 522.

84. Lindsay, *The Epic of Captain Scott*, pp. 171–72.

85. Quoted in Preston, *A First Rate Tragedy*, p. 237.

FOR FURTHER READING

Owen Beattie, *Buried in Ice*. New York: Scholastic Books, 1993. A book about John Franklin and his expedition, with emphasis on the fate of the men who sailed into the Arctic.

Martyn Bramwell, *Polar Exploration*. New York: DK Publishing, 1998. A short and well-illustrated account of exploration in the Arctic and Antarctic.

Christopher Dwyer, *Robert Peary and the Quest for North Pole*. New York: Chelsea House, 1992. Information about Peary's life and work.

Jeri Ferris, *Arctic Explorer: The Story of Matthew Henson*. Minneapolis: Carolrhoda Books, 1989. A short account of Matthew Henson's life.

Matthew Henson, *A Black Explorer at the North Pole*. New York: Walker, 1969. Authored by Henson with a ghostwriter, the book focuses on Henson's 1908–1909 journey to the North Pole.

Philip Arthur Sauvain, *Robert Scott in the Antarctic*. Minneapolis: Dillon Press, 1993. Describes Scott's life and work.

Ann and Myron Sutton, *Journey into Ice*. Chicago: Rand McNally, 1965. A book about John Franklin and his voyages that quotes extensively from Franklin's letters and journals, but also invents dialogue.

Roald Amundsen, *The North West Passage.* Vols. 1 and 2. New York: Dutton, 1908. Amundsen's account of the voyage of the *Gjøa.*

——, *The South Pole.* Vols. 1 and 2. New York: Lee Keedick, 1913. Amundsen's own description of his journey to the South Pole, including maps, charts, and scientific tables.

T. H. Baughman, *Pilgrims on the Ice.* Lincoln: University of Nebraska Press, 1999. A thorough account of Robert Scott's first Antarctic expedition, covering the years 1901–1904 written extensively about Antarctic exploration.

Pierre Berton, *The Arctic Grail: The Quest for the Northwest Passage and the North Pole, 1818–1909.* New York: Viking, 1988. Well written and exhaustively researched; the single best book available on Arctic exploration during the nineteenth and early twentieth centuries.

Scott Cookman, *Ice Blink.* New York: John Wiley and Sons, 2000. A readable description of Franklin's last voyage; Cookman's main interest is in reconstructing the movements of Franklin's men and discovering what went wrong.

S. Allen Counter, *North Pole Legacy: Black, White, and Eskimo.* Amherst: University of Massachusetts Press, 1991. Robert Peary and Matthew Henson both fathered children with Inuit women while in Greenland. This book includes biographical information on Peary, Henson, and their Inuit descendants and describes how the various family branches met during the 1980s.

Fergus Fleming, *Barrow's Boys.* New York: Atlantic Monthly Press, 1998. Describes British explorations of the nineteenth century, polar and otherwise; includes useful information on Franklin.

Alan Gurney, *The Race to the White Continent.* New York: W. W. Norton, 2000. The history of Antarctic exploration during the early years of the nineteenth century.

Wally Herbert, *The Noose of Laurels.* New York: Atheneum, 1989. A detailed analysis of Robert Peary's life and work, with special emphasis on Peary's claims of having reached the North Pole; the author is an explorer himself.

Roland Huntford, *The Last Place on Earth.* New York: Atheneum, 1986. Long and carefully researched, the book contrasts Amundsen's and Scott's journeys to the South Pole; in Huntford's view, Amundsen is much more to be admired than Scott.

Martin Lindsay, *The Epic of Captain Scott*. New York: G. P. Putnam's Sons, 1934. A short and somewhat dated description of Robert Scott's attempt to reach the South Pole; includes quotes from Scott's diaries and the letters of other members of the expedition.

Charles Neider, ed., *Antarctica*. New York: Random House, 1972. Excerpts from the writings of explorers, from James Cook to those of the mid–twentieth century.

Robert Peary, *Northward over the Great Ice*. Vol. 1. New York: Frederick A. Stokes, 1898. Peary's own descriptions of his voyages through 1897.

Diana Preston, *A First Rate Tragedy*. New York: Houghton Mifflin, 1998. A well-written and thoroughly researched account of Robert Scott's trek to the South Pole; Preston concludes that Scott had many problems of his own making but that his achievements were real and outweighed the failures.

Ann Savours, ed., *Edward Wilson: Diary of the Discovery Expedition*. New York: Humanities Press, 1967. Wilson accompanied Scott on both his Antarctic journeys; this book presents his diary entries and illustrations from the first voyage.

Francis Spufford, *I May Be Some Time: Ice and the English Imagination*. New York: St. Martin's Press, 1997. A cultural history describing British thought about the polar regions during the nineteenth and early twentieth centuries; includes information on Franklin and Scott.

Will Steger with Paul Schurke, *North to the Pole*. New York: Random House, 1987. Steger and Schurke tell about their dogsled trip to the North Pole in 1986, with some references to earlier expeditions.

Paul-Emile Victor, *Man and the Conquest of the Poles*. Trans. Scott Sullivan. New York: Simon and Schuster, 1963. An overview of polar exploration from early times to the advent of atomic submarines.

John Edward Weems, *Peary: The Explorer and the Man*. Boston: Houghton Mifflin, 1967. An enthusiastic biography of Robert Peary, based largely on his own journals and other papers.

INDEX

PICTURE CREDITS

ABOUT THE AUTHOR

Stephen Currie is the author of more than forty books, including a number of works on history and some historical fiction. Among his books for Lucent are *Life in a Wild West Show, The Olympic Games,* and *Adoption.* He is also a teacher. He grew up in Illinois and now lives with his family in upstate New York.